Macmillan
ENCYCLOPEDIA
OF SCIENCE

10

Transportation
From the Bicycle to Spacecraft

Robin Kerrod

Macmillan Publishing Company
New York

Maxwell Macmillan International Publishing Group
New York   Oxford   Singapore   Sydney

Published by:
Macmillan Publishing Company
A Division of Macmillan, Inc.
866 Third Avenue, New York, NY 10022

Collier Macmillan Canada, Inc.
1200 Eglinton Avenue East, Suite 200
Don Mills, Ontario M3C 3N1

Planned and produced by Andromeda Oxford Ltd.

Copyright © 1991 Andromeda Oxford Ltd.
Macmillan edition copyright © 1991 Macmillan Publishing Company

Library of Congress Cataloging-in-Publication Data

Macmillan encyclopedia of science.
     p.   cm.
     Includes bibliographical references and index.
     Summary: An encyclopedia of science and technology, covering
such areas as the Earth, the ocean, plants and animals, medicine,
agriculture, manufacturing, and transportation.
     ISBN 0-02-941346-X (set)
     1. Science–Encyclopedias, Juvenile.   2. Engineering–
Encyclopedias, Juvenile.   3. Technology–Encyclopedias, Juvenile.
[1. Science–Encyclopedias.   2. Technology–Encyclopedias.]
I. Macmillan Publishing Company   90-19940
Q121.M27   1991   CIP
503 – dc20   AC

Volumes of the *Macmillan Encyclopedia of Science*
 1 *Matter and Energy* ISBN 0-02-941141-6
 2 *The Heavens* ISBN 0-02-941142-4
 3 *The Earth* ISBN 0-02-941143-2
 4 *Life on Earth* ISBN 0-02-941144-0
 5 *Plants and Animals* ISBN 0-02-941145-9
 6 *Body and Health* ISBN 0-02-941146-7
 7 *The Environment* ISBN 0-02-941147-5
 8 *Industry* ISBN 0-02-941341-9
 9 *Fuel and Power* ISBN 0-02-941342-7
10 *Transportation* ISBN 0-02-941343-5
11 *Communication* ISBN 0-02-941344-3
12 *Tools and Tomorrow* ISBN 0-02-941345-1

Printed in the United States of America

Introduction

Cars and trains, airships and planes, hydrofoils and submarines – these and other means of Earth-bound transportation are dealt with in this volume, along with artificial satellites, spacecraft, and life-support systems used beyond the Earth's atmosphere. (Volume 9 discusses engines, and Volume 12 highlights transportation frontiers.)

To learn about a specific topic, start by consulting the Index at the end of the book. You can find references throughout the encyclopedia to the topic by turning to the final Index, covering all 12 volumes, located in Volume 12.

If you come across an unfamiliar word while using this book, the Glossary may be of help. A list of key abbreviations can be found on page 87. If you want to learn more about the subjects covered in the book, the Further Reading section is a good place to begin.

Scientists tend to express measurements in units belonging to the "International System," which incorporates metric units. This encyclopedia accordingly uses metric units (with American equivalents also given in the main text). More information on units of measurement is on page 86.

Contents

Part One

Travel by land, sea and air

Human beings are not by themselves physically capable of traveling fast or carrying heavy loads over long distances. So they have over the years developed ingenious methods of transportation to give them that capability over land, across the sea, and through the air.

The first great breakthroughs in transportation came with the invention of the wheel and the sailing ship, both about 5,500 years ago. But not until engines were added to ships and vehicles in the 1800s did the real revolution begin.

By the early 1900s cars were replacing the horse and buggy and beginning to transform society. At the same time machines began flying in the air, making virtually the whole world accessible for travel. Today, planes flying twice as high as Mount Everest and at twice the speed of a rifle bullet can whisk us thousands of kilometers in a few hours.

◀ A multilevel highway interchange in the city of Rotterdam, in the Netherlands. Such designs assist the speed and safety of city transportation by separating traffic traveling in opposite directions.

On the road

Spot facts

- *The Italian artist and inventor Leonardo da Vinci designed a bicycle of sorts five centuries ago. Like many of his ideas, such as the parachute and helicopter, it was way ahead of its time.*

- *Some motorcycles built for fast acceleration are able to reach speeds of more than 300 km/h (roughly 200 mph) from a standing start in less than seven seconds.*

- *The most successful car ever produced was the Volkswagen "Beetle," introduced in Germany in 1938. Twenty-one million vehicles were sold worldwide during the half-century it remained in production.*

- *Some racing cars have upside-down "wings" (inverted airfoils) to prevent their bodies and wheels from lifting at high speeds.*

▶ Cars slow to a crawl during the evening rush hour in Sydney, Australia. A similar thing happens in most other large cities the world over, causing frustration, wasting energy, and harming the environment.

The wheel is perhaps the greatest invention made by humankind. Transportation on land hinges upon the wheel and modifications of it, such as the chainwheel and sprockets on bicycles, and the gearwheels and flywheels in motorcycle, car, and truck engines.

Motor vehicles have become essential to our way of life. Cars and motorcycles give us freedom to travel when and where we want. Heavier commercial vehicles supply the needs of industry and commerce. But so many vehicles now use the streets and highways that traffic, especially in cities, is grinding to a halt, and the environment is being put at risk by the fumes their engines emit.

The wheel

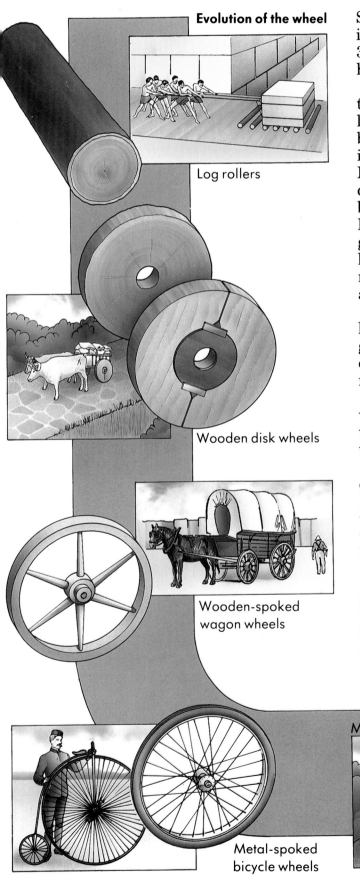

Evolution of the wheel

Log rollers

Wooden disk wheels

Wooden-spoked wagon wheels

Metal-spoked bicycle wheels

Strangely enough, the wheel was first used not in transportation, but in pottery making. About 3500 BC potters began using a rotating wheel to help them mold clay into circular shapes.

The wheel came into use for transport some time during the next 300 years. Almost certainly it was used first in Mesopotamia, the region between the Tigris and Euphrates rivers which is now in modern Iraq. A picture from Mesopotamia showing a wheeled cart has been dated at about 3200 BC. The famous decorated box known as the "Standard of Ur" (about 2500 BC) shows horse-drawn, four-wheeled carts going into battle. Their wheels were made up of half-disks of wood jointed together and mounted on axles. Pins through the ends of the axles held the wheels in place.

By the time of the Egyptian pharaoh Tutankhamen (1300s BC) the ponderous war carts had given way to light, fast, two-wheeled war chariots with slim, spoked wheels. The rim was made of wood, bent by being heated in a fire.

In Roman times the cart and chariot wheel was improved by fitting an iron band around the rim. This kind of wagon wheel survived into the present century.

Wire-spoke wheels with solid rubber tires came into use on bicycles in the 1870s. By the 1890s, pneumatic (air-filled) tires were being used with both bicycles and the early cars. Car wheels today are made of steel or alloys and have multilayered tires.

◄ Before the invention of the wheel, people moved heavy loads by rolling them along on logs. The first wheels were made from disks sliced from logs. Spoked wheels remained in use for some 4,000 years and have only recently been superseded by solid metal ones.

Modern metal wheel

Radial-ply tire

The bicycle

The bicycle, or bike, is the most efficient form of mechanical transportation yet devised. It needs no fuel to run, is easy to ride, and requires little maintenance. Scientists are not really certain why riding and balancing on a bike is so easy. Some think the bike stays stable because of the gyroscopic action of the spinning wheels, but others feel that this is only part of the story.

The bike has been around in more or less its modern form for about a century. It has a diamond-shaped frame and two wheels of equal size. It is driven by the rear wheel through an endless chain, which connects with a chainwheel, a large gear wheel, or sprocket, turned by the rider pushing on the pedals. The chainwheel and pedals form a crank system, which converts the up-and-down movement of the rider's legs into rotary motion. (An automobile engine uses a crankshaft to do this.)

To make it easier to climb hills, most bikes have gears. The first kinds of gears used were hub gears, built into the hub of the rear wheel. A hub gear is a type known as an epicyclic, or sun-and-planet gear. It comprises a central large gear wheel (sun), with two smaller ones (planets) meshing with it. In turn the planets mesh with the inside of a toothed ring (annulus). By keeping any of these components stationary, the others can be made to rotate at different speeds. This principle is applied to make the wheel turn at different speeds for the same chain speed.

Most modern bikes, however, have derailleur gears. They have a set of sprockets of different sizes fixed to the rear wheel hub. The chain leads from the chainwheel to the rear sprocket through a spring-guide mechanism. The gear-shift lever moves an arm sideways. This transfers the chain to a different-sized rear sprocket and makes the wheel turn faster (smaller sprocket) or slower (larger sprocket) for the same chain speed.

Some bikes have two chainwheels – two different-sized front sprockets with a chain-moving mechanism above. Moving the chain from one to the other doubles the number of gears at the rear. Some mountain and other bikes have a triple chainwheel and six gears on the rear sprockets, making 18 gears. These help them negotiate steep slopes and other obstacles.

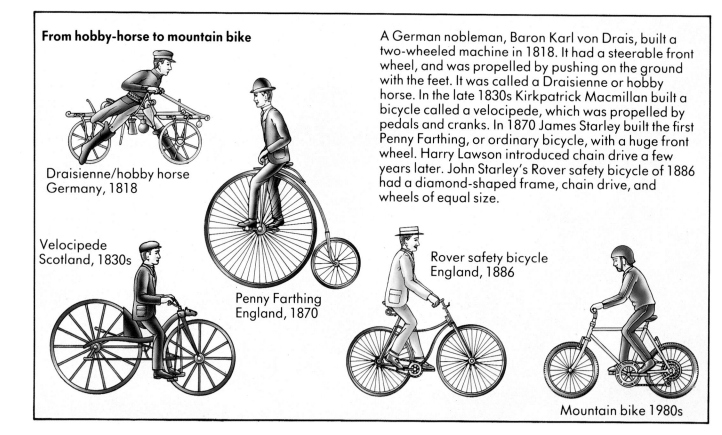

From hobby-horse to mountain bike

Draisienne/hobby horse
Germany, 1818

Velocipede
Scotland, 1830s

Penny Farthing
England, 1870

A German nobleman, Baron Karl von Drais, built a two-wheeled machine in 1818. It had a steerable front wheel, and was propelled by pushing on the ground with the feet. It was called a Draisienne or hobby horse. In the late 1830s Kirkpatrick Macmillan built a bicycle called a velocipede, which was propelled by pedals and cranks. In 1870 James Starley built the first Penny Farthing, or ordinary bicycle, with a huge front wheel. Harry Lawson introduced chain drive a few years later. John Starley's Rover safety bicycle of 1886 had a diamond-shaped frame, chain drive, and wheels of equal size.

Rover safety bicycle
England, 1886

Mountain bike 1980s

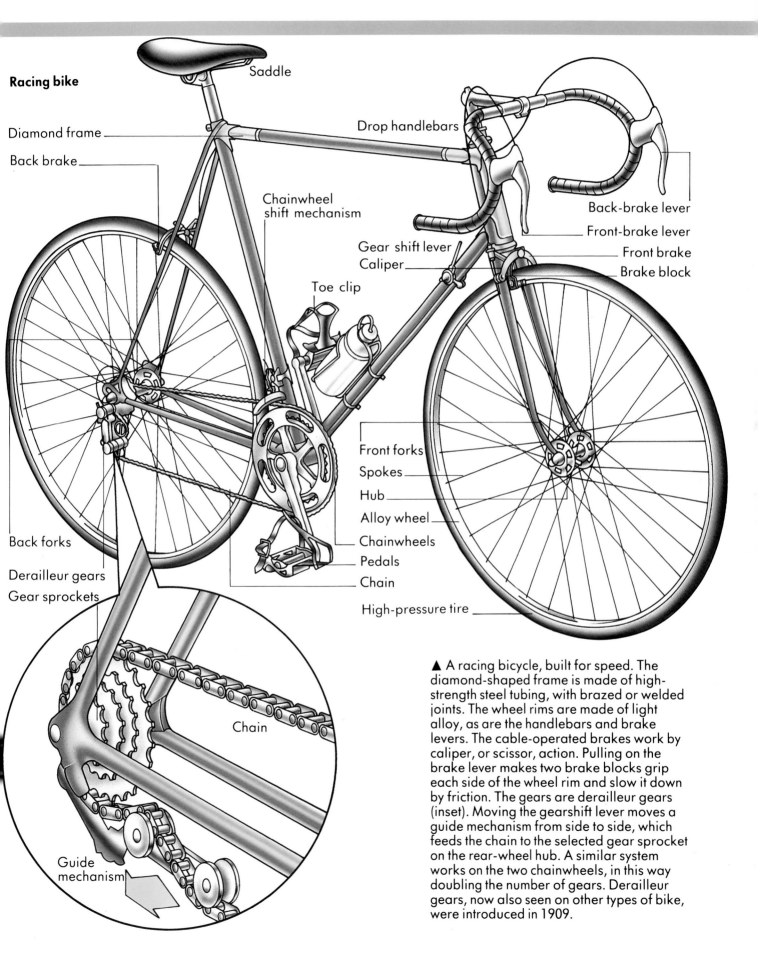

Racing bike

Saddle

Diamond frame

Back brake

Drop handlebars

Chainwheel shift mechanism

Gear shift lever
Caliper

Back-brake lever

Front-brake lever

Front brake

Brake block

Toe clip

Front forks

Spokes

Hub

Alloy wheel

Chainwheels

Pedals

Chain

High-pressure tire

Back forks

Derailleur gears
Gear sprockets

Chain

Guide mechanism

▲ A racing bicycle, built for speed. The diamond-shaped frame is made of high-strength steel tubing, with brazed or welded joints. The wheel rims are made of light alloy, as are the handlebars and brake levers. The cable-operated brakes work by caliper, or scissor, action. Pulling on the brake lever makes two brake blocks grip each side of the wheel rim and slow it down by friction. The gears are derailleur gears (inset). Moving the gearshift lever moves a guide mechanism from side to side, which feeds the chain to the selected gear sprocket on the rear-wheel hub. A similar system works on the two chainwheels, in this way doubling the number of gears. Derailleur gears, now also seen on other types of bike, were introduced in 1909.

The motorcycle

The motorcycle combines features of both the bicycle and the car. The frame is broadly similar to that of a bicycle, with the front wheel held in forks, which are turned by the handlebars for steering. The power from the engine is usually carried by chain to a sprocket on the rear wheel. A few models, however, have shaft drive.

The standard motorcycle engine is a gasoline engine that works on the four-stroke cycle like an automobile engine. Smaller motorcycles may have a two-stroke engine, which is simpler in design and easier to maintain. In most motorcycles the engine is air-cooled: fins around the engine cylinders give a greater area for cooling.

As in an automobile, engine power is controlled by a throttle and transmitted through a clutch and transmission. The rider's right hand is used to work the twist-grip throttle, which increases or decreases engine speed by allowing more, or less, fuel mixture into the engine cylinders. The clutch is operated by a lever on the left handlebar; the transmission by a gearshift pedal, also on the left.

A motorcycle may have drum or disk brakes, or a combination of the two. Applying the brakes forces brake shoes or pads against a drum or disk attached to the wheel. The front brake is applied by means of a hand lever on the right handlebar, while the rear brake is applied by means of a foot pedal, also on the right.

Anatomy of a superbike

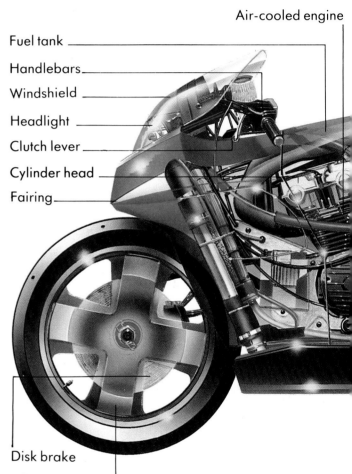

Air-cooled engine

Fuel tank

Handlebars

Windshield

Headlight

Clutch lever

Cylinder head

Fairing

Disk brake

Alloy wheel

From steam bike to superbike

Ernest and Pierre Michaux (France) built a steam-powered motorcycle in 1868. Gottlieb Daimler (Germany) developed the first gasoline-driven machine in 1885, before turning his attention to motor cars. The modern form of the motorcycle appeared in 1901, designed by Michael and Eugene Werner (France). It had the engine slung low down between the wheels and used a twist-grip throttle. Motorcycle manufacturers sprang up: for example, Norton, BSA, and Matchless in Great Britain, Indian in the United States, and BMW in Germany. In the 1950s, motor scooters like the Vespa became popular. Since then Japanese makes, such as Honda, Suzuki, Yamaha, and Kawasaki, have come to dominate the scene.

Michaux steam bike
France, 1868

Daimler original
Germany, 1885

Sunbeam
England,
1914

▼ The modern superbike has a powerful engine and breathtaking performance. On the track it can reach speeds up to 250 km/h (over 150 mph). Its body has a streamlined fairing to reduce air resistance. Disk brakes on both wheels ensure efficient and safe braking.

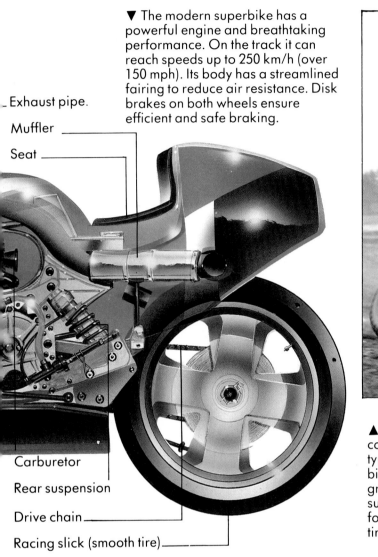

Exhaust pipe.

Muffler

Seat

Carburetor

Rear suspension

Drive chain

Racing slick (smooth tire)

▲ A motocross rider hustling his bike around a cross-country course. The machines used for motocross, a type of dirt-track racing, are rugged lightweight bikes, usually with a two-stroke engine. The high ground clearance of the body allows for excessive suspension movement over the rough, bumpy ground found on motocross courses. The motorcycles have tires with a chunky tread, which give them good grip.

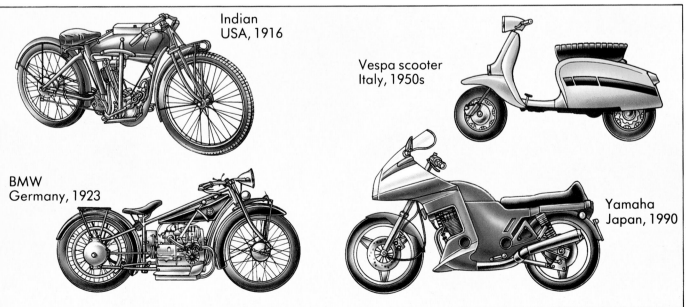

Indian
USA, 1916

Vespa scooter
Italy, 1950s

BMW
Germany, 1923

Yamaha
Japan, 1990

Automobile systems

The automobile is made up of as many as 14,000 different parts. These are assembled into larger components, which in turn are put together on the automobile production line. It is convenient to describe a car in terms of the systems that are needed to make it run. The engine unit forms one major system, and itself comprises many subsystems: fuel, ignition, lubrication, cooling, and so on. The engine power is carried to the driving wheels by the power train.

In the conventional automobile layout shown here, the power train is made up of the clutch, transmission, drive shaft, and final drive. The clutch connects with the flywheel of the engine and cuts off power to the transmission when the driver wants to change gear.

When the gearshift lever is moved, different sets of gear wheels in the transmission mesh together to increase or decrease the speed of the output shaft. The drive shaft carries the motion to the differential, which transfers the motion to the axle shafts that turn the wheels.

A variety of other systems help the driver control the car. He or she guides it through the steering system and slows it down using the braking system. The foot brake works hydraulically and acts on all four wheels. The parking brake works mechanically and acts on only the rear wheels. The automobile also has a suspension system to cushion passengers from jarring on bad road surfaces.

▶ The major systems in this conventionally designed automobile are color-coded. The engine, exhaust, and fuel tanks, are violet. So is the power train system of clutch, transmission, drive shaft, and final drive. The cooling system, which uses the radiator to cool hot water circulating from the engine, is blue. The braking system, which comprises disk brakes at the front and drum brakes at the rear, is pink. So is the suspension system, which incorporates springs and shock absorbers. The electrical system, comprising the battery, coil, distributor, alternator, lights, windshield wipers, and instruments, is orange.

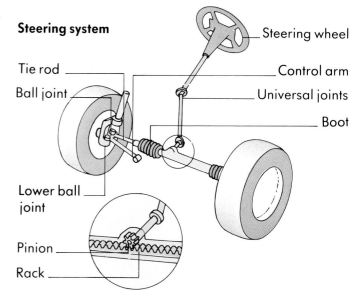

Steering system

Steering wheel
Tie rod
Ball joint
Control arm
Universal joints
Boot
Lower ball joint
Pinion
Rack

▲ This kind of steering system is called rack-and-pinion. Turning the steering wheel rotates a small gear wheel, or pinion. This moves the toothed rack from side to side. The rack is linked to the front wheels by a pair of tie rods.

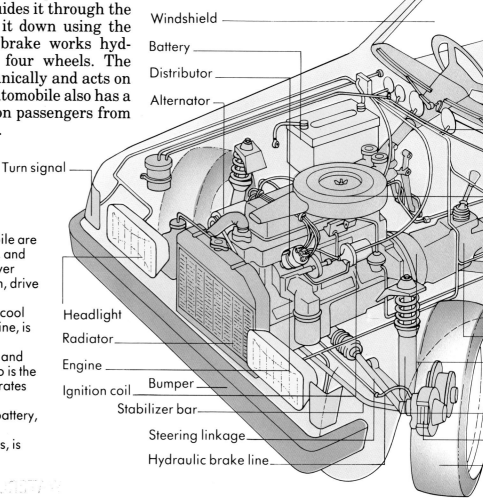

Windshield
Battery
Distributor
Alternator
Turn signal
Headlight
Radiator
Engine
Ignition coil
Bumper
Stabilizer bar
Steering linkage
Hydraulic brake line

► The clutch, transmission and differential are key units in the power train. The clutch is mounted on the engine flywheel. The pressure plate forces the clutch plate against the flywheel to transmit motion to the transmission. It is sprung away from the driven plate when the clutch pedal is depressed. The purpose of the transmission is to mesh different-sized gear wheels and change the speed of the output shaft. The design of the differential allows the two drive wheels to turn at different speeds and thus prevent skidding when cornering. In drum brakes the linings are forced against a drum attached to the wheel and slow it down by friction. In disk brakes the brake pads are forced against a disk attached to the wheel.

Layout of a rear-wheel drive car

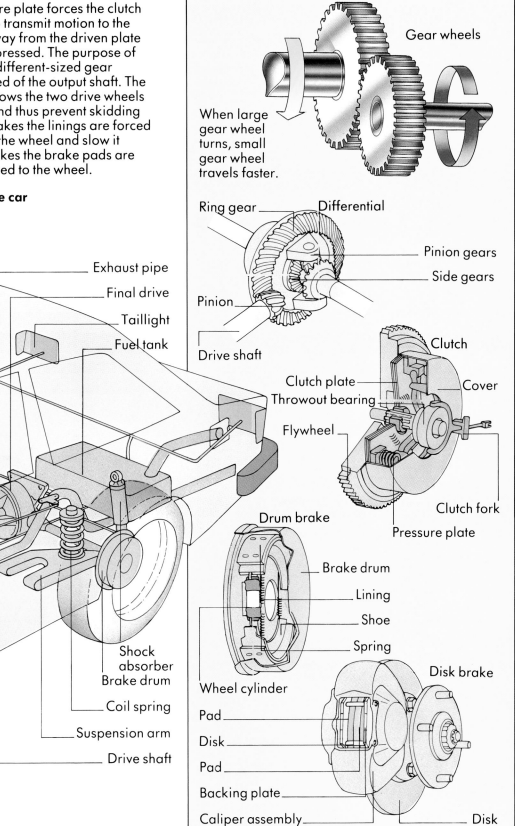

Power train and brakes

Gear wheels

When large gear wheel turns, small gear wheel travels faster.

Ring gear — Differential

Pinion gears

Side gears

Pinion

Drive shaft

Clutch

Clutch plate — Cover

Throwout bearing

Flywheel

Clutch fork

Pressure plate

Drum brake

Brake drum

Lining

Shoe

Spring

Wheel cylinder

Pad

Disk

Pad

Backing plate

Caliper assembly

Disk brake

Disk

Body

Exhaust pipe

Final drive

Steering wheel

Taillight

Windshield wiper

Fuel tank

Instruments

Air filter

Shock absorber

Brake cable

Brake drum

Transmission

Coil spring

Clutch housing

Suspension arm

Drive shaft

Front suspension

Disk brake

Tire

Automobile design

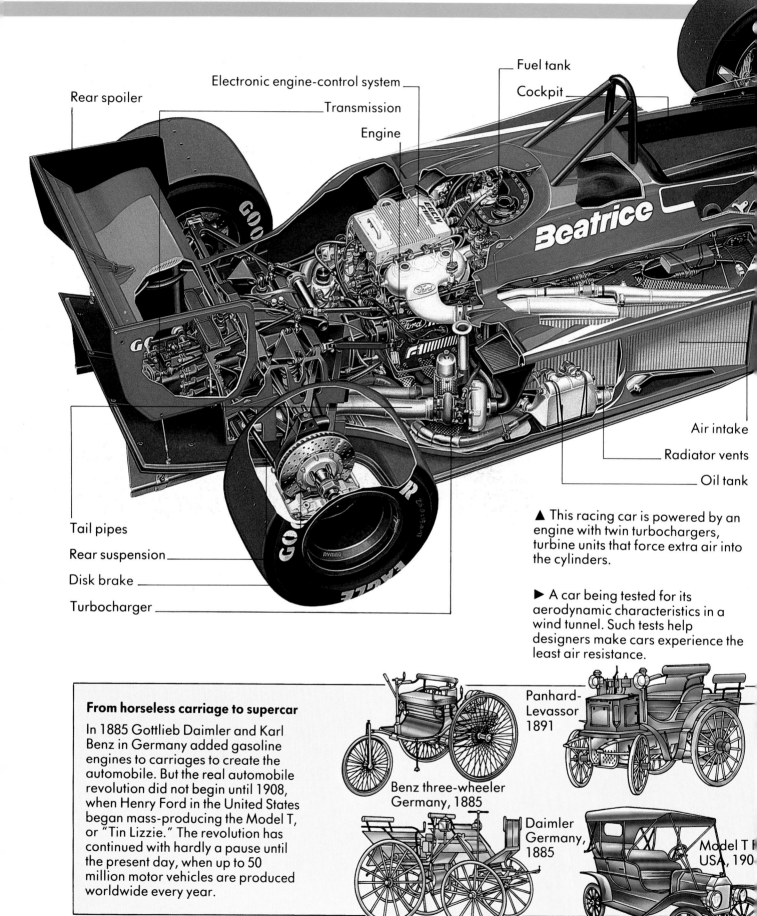

Rear spoiler

Electronic engine-control system

Transmission

Engine

Fuel tank

Cockpit

Beatrice

Air intake

Radiator vents

Oil tank

Tail pipes

Rear suspension

Disk brake

Turbocharger

▲ This racing car is powered by an engine with twin turbochargers, turbine units that force extra air into the cylinders.

▶ A car being tested for its aerodynamic characteristics in a wind tunnel. Such tests help designers make cars experience the least air resistance.

From horseless carriage to supercar

In 1885 Gottlieb Daimler and Karl Benz in Germany added gasoline engines to carriages to create the automobile. But the real automobile revolution did not begin until 1908, when Henry Ford in the United States began mass-producing the Model T, or "Tin Lizzie." The revolution has continued with hardly a pause until the present day, when up to 50 million motor vehicles are produced worldwide every year.

Benz three-wheeler Germany, 1885

Panhard-Levassor 1891

Daimler Germany, 1885

Model T F USA, 190

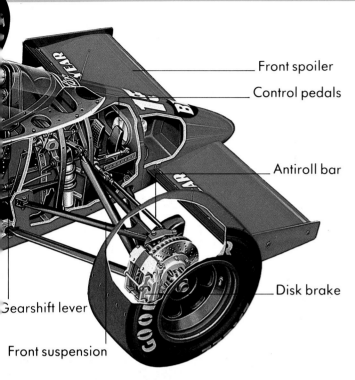

Front spoiler

Control pedals

Antiroll bar

Disk brake

Gearshift lever

Front suspension

In a little over a century the automobile has evolved from a crude motorized horseless carriage into a sophisticated machine that is sleek, swift, and comfortable. Car designs have changed markedly both inside and out as the years have gone by. Methods and materials of construction have altered. Engines have been progressively improved to be more economical and, in recent years, to reduce pollution. Diesel engines, once used only for trucks and buses, are now sometimes found in cars. They last longer, use cheaper fuel, and provide more economical motoring.

The most obvious feature of car design is body shape, which varies according to the type of car (sedan, hatchback, station wagon, coupe, convertible) and from manufacturer to manufacturer. Until the 1950s most car bodies were built by attaching body panels to a rigid frame, or chassis. Since then one-piece, or unit, construction has been the norm. In this method the body is put together as a "shell" of shaped welded steel panels.

The automobile is a lethal weapon if it is in the hands of a bad driver or gets out of control. Designers bear this in mind, and incorporate as many safety features as possible. They try to build the passenger compartment as a "safety cage" so that it is rigid enough to remain intact if the car crashes. They build "crumple zones" into the front and rear of the car to absorb much of the energy of an impact there. The doors may be reinforced with steel bars to prevent them from caving in. Designers conduct crash tests to see how safe their designs are in practice.

Rolls-Royce
Great Britain, 1909

Volkswagen (VW)
Germany, 1938

Mini
Great Britain, 1960s

Lamborghini
Italy, 1970s

Citroen
France, 1934

Pontiac
USA, 1950s

17

Commercial vehicles

In business and industry the efficient transporting of raw materials, products, and goods is essential to keep production lines busy and customers happy. For such transportation a wide variety of different vehicles are made, from light vans carrying office supplies to heavy trucks carrying gravel from quarries. These freight carriers are known as commercial vehicles. In most countries, particularly the United States, trucking – carrying goods by truck – is big business.

Apart from freight carriers, there are many other kinds of commercial vehicles, for example buses to carry passengers over short and long distances; garbage trucks to remove household trash; fire engines to fight fires; and rotating mixer trucks to carry wet cement to building sites.

Although these vehicles are very different in function and appearance, underneath they are basically similar. They are based on an engine and chassis unit. They differ in the type of bodywork added to this unit. Usually the engine is a diesel, a rugged engine that runs on diesel oil. For extra power, it might be turbocharged, which means that extra air is forced into the engine cylinders by a turbocharger.

Commercial vehicles that haul heavy loads require a transmission with many more gears than a car so that they can cope with hills and different road conditions. A common arrange-

◄ One of the fire trucks of the town of Stonington, Maine. It has a special body on a standard two-axle chassis. It carries escape ladders and has built-in pumps for forcing water through the fire hoses.

► Double-decker buses like this provide efficient, high-volume in-town transportation. This is a Super Metrobus, now in service in Hong Kong with the Kowloon Motor Company. It is 12 m (40 ft.) long and can carry up to 170 passengers. It has a turbocharged diesel engine and automatic transmission. The body is made of aluminum, and the passengers enjoy a comfortable ride because of the air suspension.

◄ A tractor-trailer passing through a small town in New England. The tractor unit has three axles with four wheels on the rear two. It has the distinctive vertical muffler and exhaust pipe of the American truck. Like all heavy trucks, it has powerful air brakes, applied using air compressed by an engine-driven compressor.

▼ A dump truck removes a load of rock from a quarry in northern England. It is a rugged, off-the-road vehicle with large, chunky tires, and all four rear wheels are powered to give extra traction over rough terrain. The hydraulic ram that tips the body is clearly visible. Dump trucks are also widely used in the construction of roads.

ment is to have two transmissions in tandem: a main transmission with up to six forward gears and one reverse, and an auxiliary transmission with two gears, making 14 gears in all.

The smaller commercial vehicles have just two wheel axles, like a car. Bigger ones may have as many as four axles to distribute their load more evenly. In these the front two axles are used for steering, and the rear two are both drive axles.

Other vehicles are "articulated". The power unit, or tractor, is separate from the load-carrying part, the semitrailer. The two parts connect via a coupling called a fifth wheel, which allows them to swivel independently. This arrangement makes for easier maneuvering and greater flexibility of operation: any tractor is able to haul any semitrailer.

Trains

- *The standard gauge of railroad track – the distance the rails are apart – is 143.5 cm (4 ft., 8½ in.) The other most common gauge is the meter gauge (3.28 ft.).*

- *The largest steam locomotives ever built were Union Pacific Railroad's "Big Boys." They weighed no less than 600 metric tons, had 16 driving wheels, and had the pull of over 6,000 horses.*

- *Japan has the busiest railroad system in the world, carrying over 20 million passengers daily.*

- *London has the world's oldest (from 1863) and most extensive subway system, with over 400 km (250 mi.) of track, of which more than a third is in deep tunnels.*

- *A French train, the TGV, broke the rail speed record with a run of 515.3 km/h (320.2 mph) in April 1990.*

- ▶ *An electric locomotive hauls an express train through the scenic Rhine Valley in Germany. German Railways (Deutsche Bundesbahn) maintains one of the world's most efficient rail networks.*

The coming of the railroads in the early part of the 1800s brought about a revolution in transportation. On the "iron road" people could travel long distances in comparative comfort, speed, and safety for the first time. For more than a century steam locomotives hauled the trains, but more efficient electric and diesel locomotives have since taken over. The advantage of the railroad for transportation is that it can carry enormous loads, of passengers or freight, and make very efficient use of fuel. This is because there is minimal friction between the steel wheels of the trains and the steel track they run on.

The Railroad Age

In 1804 Richard Trevithick put a steam engine on rails to create the first railroad locomotive. But the Railroad Age did not really begin until 1825. In that year the British engineer George Stephenson completed the first public steam railroad, the Stockton and Darlington Railway. Five years later he built the Liverpool and Manchester Railway, and also the locomotive that hauled the first train on it, the *Rocket*. Railroad mania began to spread worldwide.

In the USA the railroads opened up new territories for settlement: in 1869 the first transcontinental railroad was completed, worked by American Standard locomotives, with huge smokestack and cowcatcher. By the 1930s in Great Britain streamlined locomotives like the *Mallard* were setting speed records in excess of 200 km/h (125 mph). In the United States in the 1940s monster locomotives like Union Pacific's "Big Boys" were being built, exceeding 600 metric tons in weight. But the days of steam were ending. Diesel and electric locomotives were taking over.

Trevithick's locomotive
Great Britain, 1804

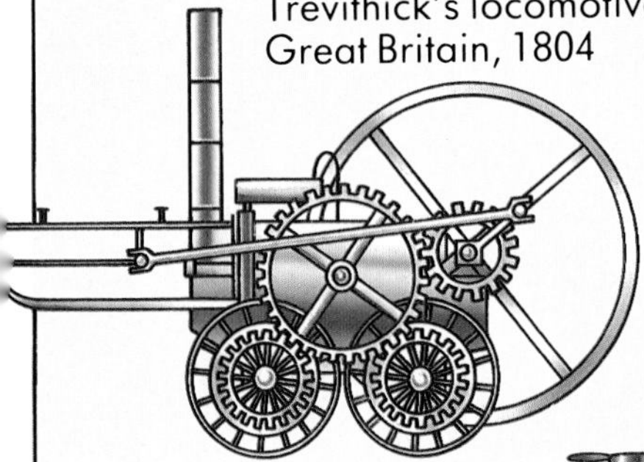

American Standard Locomotive
USA, 1860s

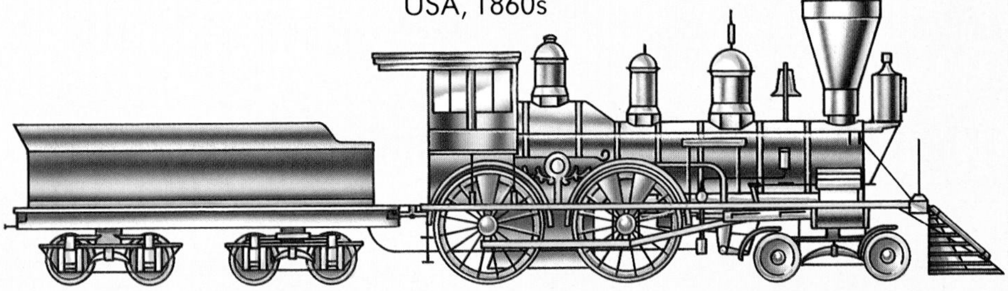

Snowdon Mountain Railway
Wales, 1896

Bavarian State Railway, 1908

Union Pacific Big Boy
USA, 1941

Mallard
Great Britain, 1938

Union Pacific Centennial 6900
USA, 1950s

Shinkansen bullet train Japan, 1964

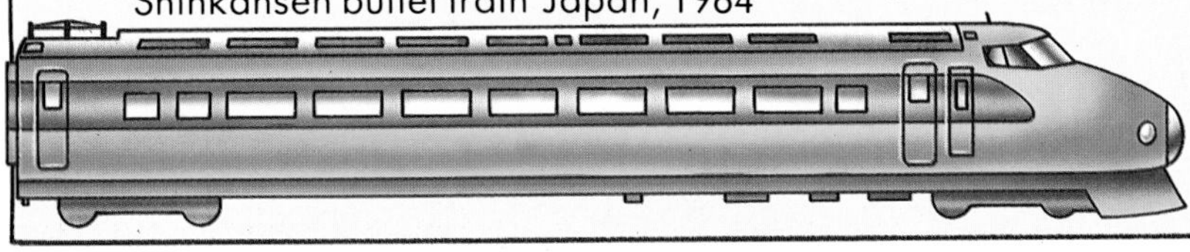

Bay Area Rapid Transit (BART)
USA, 1970s

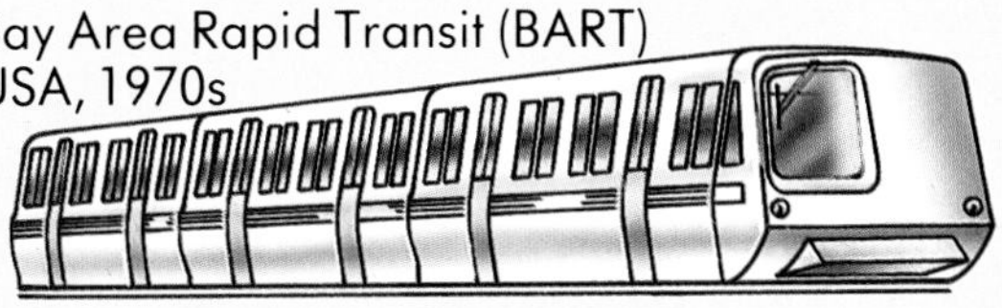

Locomotives

Two main kinds of locomotives haul modern trains: electric and diesel. Electric locomotives are the most common type in Europe; they were introduced into mainline service in Italy in the 1920s. Diesels are particularly popular in the United States. Streamlined diesel passenger trains were introduced there in the mid-1930s, shortly after Germany's *Flying Hamburger* train (1932) had pioneered diesel passenger travel.

Diesels use the same kind of piston engine as heavy trucks, and burn diesel oil as fuel. They are known as compression-ignition engines. This is because the fuel ignites when it is injected into hot, highly compressed air in the cylinders. Otherwise, the engines operate in the same way as automobile gasoline engines.

Engine power may be transmitted to a diesel locomotive's driving wheels in three main ways. In diesel-electric locomotives, the engine drives an electricity generator. Then the current that is produced is fed to electric motors, which turn the driving wheels. Diesel-hydraulic locomotives use a kind of liquid coupling between the engine and the wheels. Diesel-

Preserved steam

Steam locomotives have in most countries been relegated to the history books, although examples can still be seen working in Eastern Europe, South America, and India. In other countries, steam railroads are kept alive by bands of dedicated enthusiasts. They rescue and repair abandoned locomotives and run them on preserved lines that they have bought.

Great Britain is at the forefront of steam-locomotive preservation, as befits the country where the railroads were first developed. One of the star attractions at "living-steam" displays is the *Flying Scotsman* (right), a renowned Pacific Class locomotive, which was built in 1923. In 1934 it became the first locomotive in the world to reach a speed of 100 miles an hour (160 km/h). In its 40-year working life, it traveled more than 3,300,000 km (2 million mi.)

Electric locomotive

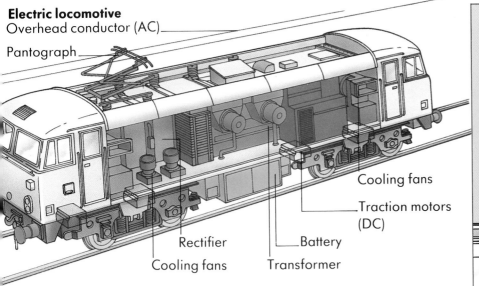

Overhead conductor (AC)

Pantograph

Rectifier

Cooling fans

Cooling fans

Traction motors (DC)

Battery

Transformer

Third-rail system

Some electric locomotives receive current not from an overhead conductor, but from a third, insulated rail laid alongside the ordinary track. They are equipped with a "shoe" that slides along the third rail. Some mainline railroads and many subways use the third-rail system, operating on DC.

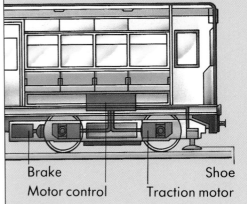

Brake

Motor control

Shoe

Traction motor

◄ Two diesel-electric locomotives head a freight train on the Union Pacific Railroad in the western United States. They are among the most powerful diesels in the world, with a power output of over 6,500 horsepower. As many as four diesel units may be used in the West to haul freight trains measuring several kilometres long.

▲ A mainline electric locomotive operating on a 25,000-volt alternating current (AC) supply. The pantograph picks up current from the overhead conductor and feeds it to a transformer, which reduces the voltage. Next, the current is converted to direct current (DC) by a rectifier and fed to the traction motors that drive the wheels.

mechanical locomotives, mainly used for shunting, have a mechanical transmission, rather like a truck.

Electric locomotives are very clean, quiet, and pollution-free and highly efficient. Their main drawback is that they can run only on special track, whereas diesels can run on any track. On most electrified track, the locomotives pick up electricity from an overhead line, or conductor. They carry on top a spring-held arm, or pantograph, which makes contact with the conductor. Other electric locomotives pick up current from a third rail.

Most of the world's overhead conductor systems operate at a voltage of 25,000 volts AC (alternating current). On the locomotive, this voltage is typically first reduced by a transformer, and then converted to DC (direct current) by a rectifier. The current is fed to DC motors, which drive the wheels.

There are also a few gas-turbine locomotives in some countries, notably the United States, Canada, the Soviet Union, and France. They are propelled by a turbine spun by hot gas.

High-speed trains

In most countries the railroads were first built 150 or more years ago. Over the years track has been improved by using more rigid concrete sleepers, or supports, and by the use of continuous welded rails, often several kilometers long. The use of such rails makes for a smoother and quieter ride. It eliminates the relentless "clickety-clack" noise and vibration produced when wheels ran over the regular joints between the once-common shorter lengths of rail.

Nevertheless, because of curves and slight grades on most tracks, trains cannot usually average a high speed, no matter how powerful the locomotive used. To achieve consistent high speeds, special tracks need to be built. And this is what has happened in Japan and France. Tracks are built as straight and as flat as possible and have no crossing points with old tracks and few, if any, signals.

Train a Grande Vitesse (TGV)

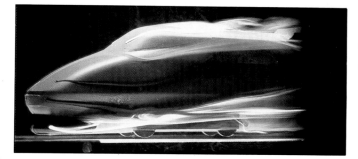

▲▼ The severely streamlined shape of the TGV (below) was designed after extensive testing of models in a high-speed wind tunnel (above).

Key

1 Collision protection
2 Brake gear
3 Driver's cab
4 Cooling air vents
5 Traction motors
6 Driver's cab air-conditioning
7 Battery compartments
8 Main transformer
9 Suspension
10 Main compressor
11 Pantograph (1,500V DC)
12 Pantograph (25,000V AC)
13 Overhead wires
14 Rectifiers
15 Baggage compartment
16 Automatic exterior doors
17 Passenger compartment
18 Inter-car bogie

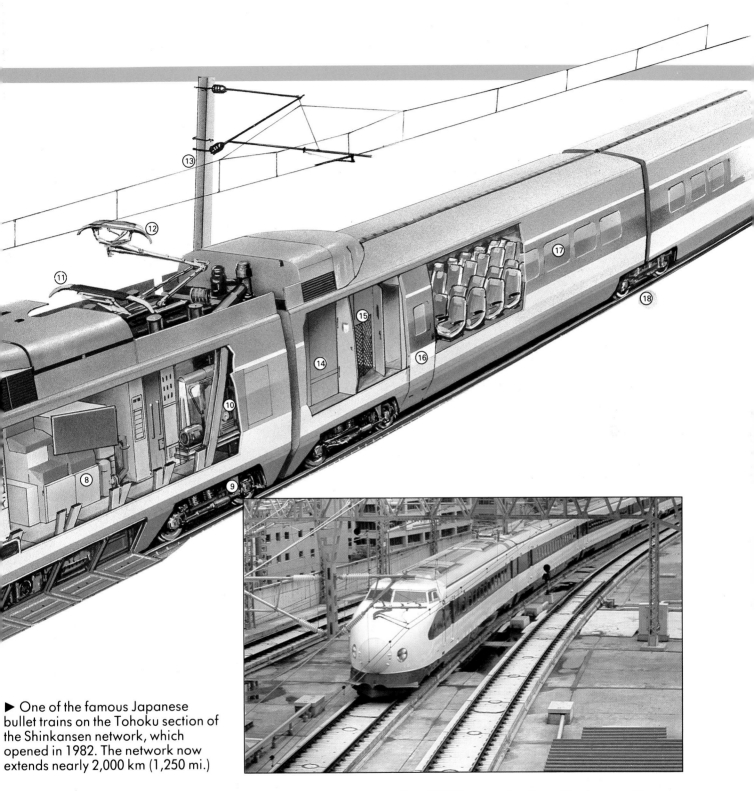

▶ One of the famous Japanese bullet trains on the Tohoku section of the Shinkansen network, which opened in 1982. The network now extends nearly 2,000 km (1,250 mi.)

Japan pioneered such rail "expressways" as long ago as 1964, when its Shinkansen, or new trunk line, opened. The first section, the New Tokaido line, ran between Tokyo and Osaka. It was operated by the streamlined, futuristic-looking "bullet trains." These electric trains achieved *average* speeds of over 160 km/h (100 mph). The network has since expanded west to Hakata and north to Niigata and Morioka.

The Shinkansen has now been surpassed as far as speed is concerned by France's TGV network. TGV stands for Train à Grande Vitesse, meaning high-speed train. And it is an apt name, for the trains regularly travel at speeds up to 290 km/h (180 mph). The first stretch of newly built track opened in 1981, between Paris and Lyons, in southeast France. The trains regularly make this 400-km (250 mi.) journey in about two hours. Like the bullet trains, the TGVs form an integrated structure of power units and passenger cars, the whole of which is streamlined to reduce air resistance.

Special railroads

Ordinary railroad track must be built as flat as possible. If it slopes too much, the wheels cannot grip the rails properly and start to slip. Yet in the European Alps and other mountainous parts of the world, some railroads climb grades as steep as 50 percent: for every 2 m of horizontal distance the track rises 1 m.

One type is the rack railroad, which uses a rack-and-pinion system to climb. There is a rack, or toothed rail, laid between the two rails of the usual track. The passenger cars have two pinions, or cogwheels, fitted underneath, which engage the teeth of the rack. Other mountain railroads are hauled by cable using a powerful winch. They often work in pairs on a funicular system: one going up as the other goes down.

Underground railroads, or subways, are the quickest method of transportation in many cities. Those in London, Paris, and New York are among the oldest underground systems; those in Washington and Hong Kong are among the newest and are highly automated. Most subway trains are electric and pick up their electricity from a third rail. The power units are incorporated in the passenger cars.

San Francisco's cable cars

The famous cable cars of San Francisco, in California, operate on a unique drive system. In a slot beneath the track runs a moving cable. Each cable car has a hand-operated clutch, which grips the cable when applied, and the car is hauled along.

Railroad operation

Passenger travel is served by the fastest trains and is the most obvious side of railroad operation. But it is not the most profitable. On most railroads freight traffic provides most of the income. And for moving goods in bulk, long distance, the railroads are unbeatable.

All manner of freight is carried by rail in a variety of freight cars: coal in gondola cars; oil in tanker cars; fruit in refrigerated cars; and trailers and containers on flat cars.

Containerization – transporting goods in standard-sized containers – is becoming increasingly common. Specialized handling equipment operates at container terminals at truck depots, stations and ports to transfer containers between truck, railroad and ship.

On busy railroad routes, especially in the morning and evening rush hours, trains follow one another along the same track with only minutes between them. This creates very real safety problems, and so over the years various traffic control systems have evolved. These days regional computerized control centers plan and monitor traffic movements of hundreds of trains over hundreds of kilometers of track. They control the signals and the switching of trains to different lines. They follow the progress of each train on a miniature track layout. Positional information is provided by electrical relays along the track, known as track circuits.

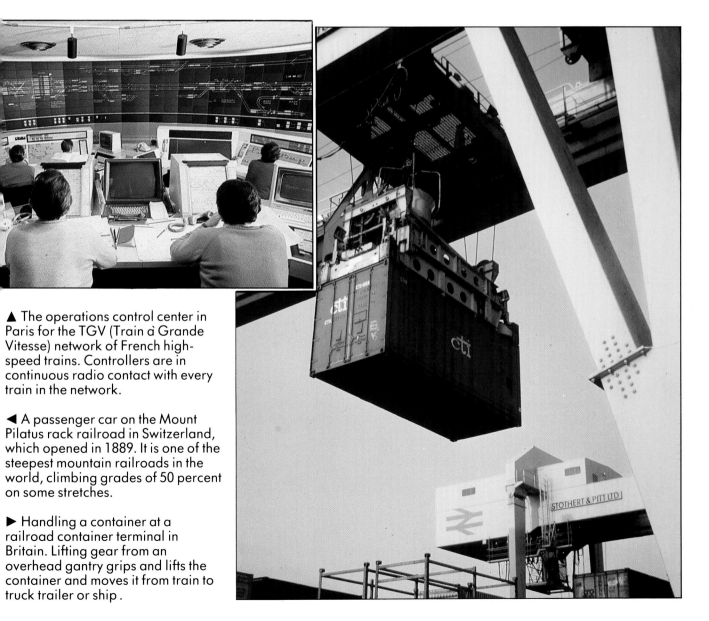

▲ The operations control center in Paris for the TGV (Train à Grande Vitesse) network of French high-speed trains. Controllers are in continuous radio contact with every train in the network.

◄ A passenger car on the Mount Pilatus rack railroad in Switzerland, which opened in 1889. It is one of the steepest mountain railroads in the world, climbing grades of 50 percent on some stretches.

► Handling a container at a railroad container terminal in Britain. Lifting gear from an overhead gantry grips and lifts the container and moves it from train to truck trailer or ship.

Ships and submarines

The wooden sailing ship vies with the horse-drawn wagon as being the oldest form of transportation. Throughout history ships have been used for commerce (merchant ships) and for fighting (naval ships), as they are still. A wide variety of ships sail the seas today, from tiny fishing boats and tugs to monster tankers, some longer than three football fields laid end to end. Under the surface lurk the most formidable of fighting vessels, nuclear submarines, powered by nuclear reactors and armed with nuclear missiles. Skimming over the surface are novel craft such as hydrofoils and hovercraft. With their hull out of the water, these surface skimmers have speeded up water transportation dramatically.

► With colorful spinnakers deployed, oceangoing yachts run before the wind. Sails provided the main form of propulsion on water until about a century and a half ago.

Development of ships

From sail to steam

The ancient Egyptians were sailing square-sailed boats on the Nile River at least 6,000 years ago. By 1000 BC the Greeks were sailing to war in fast ships called triremes, which had three banks of oars. The Vikings used sail and oars in their longships of the 900s AD. By the 1400s ships had adopted the stern rudder and the triangular lateen sail, which enabled them to sail close to the wind. Three-masted vessels carrying a combination of square and lateen sails became standard. They included the *Golden Hind*, the ship of the English explorer and adventurer Francis Drake. By the mid-1800s the speed merchants of the oceans were the great clippers. But the Age of Sail was all but over. Steamships began to appear. The *Great Britain* pioneered modern ship design, with its iron hull and screw propeller, although it still sported sails as well as a steam engine. Charles Parsons's *Turbinia* introduced steam-turbine propulsion, now used by many large vessels, such as the world's longest liner, the *Norway*, over 315 m (1,035 ft.).

Nile boat
Ancient Egypt

Trireme
Ancient Greece

The Ark Royal
England, 1587

Viking longship
AD 900s

Clipper
England/USA
1850s

Great Britain
England, 1845

United States
USA, 1952

Turbinia
England, 1897

Ship shapes

Trading ships have sailed the seas for more than 5,000 years. And they are nearly as important today as ever, despite competition from the air. The ship may be very much slower than the plane, but it can carry very much greater amounts of cargo very much more cheaply.

For carrying passengers over a long distance, the ship now takes second place. The most common working passenger ships are ferries on short sea crossings. The days of the transatlantic passenger liner are long gone. Most liners today operate as cruise ships, transporting tourists to sunny and exotic locations, such as the Mediterranean and the Caribbean.

Ships vary widely in design, according to their use. Passenger liners are easily recognized by their extensive superstructure – the part of the hull above the main deck level. They can be much like floating towns, with swimming pools, shops, restaurants, and theaters.

In contrast cargo ships, or freighters, have little superstructure. There is usually just the

▲ A freighter fully laden with standard-sized containers, which are loaded and unloaded at special container terminals. The container method of carrying freight allows goods of all types, shapes, and sizes to be transported with minimum handling problems.

Screw propeller

Practically all ships are driven by propeller, called a screw because it moves in a helical motion like a screw through the water. The Swedish-born engineer John Ericsson developed the propeller in 1836. It soon replaced the paddle wheel.

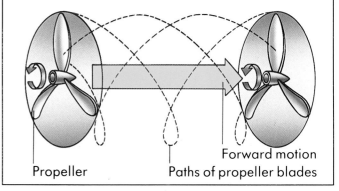

Propeller   Paths of propeller blades   Forward motion

navigation bridge and the smokestack, below which are the boilers and engines. Most of the vessel is taken up by the cargo space. In tankers, for example, this space consists of several separate tanks. They have to be separate to prevent massive surging of the oil when the ship pitches and rolls. This could readily cause the ship to capsize.

Freighters carrying mixed cargo can usually be recognized by the rows of mastlike derricks, or cranes, on deck. More specialized freighters include Ro-Ro (roll-on, roll-off) vessels. They carry trucks and trailers, which are driven on at one port and off at another. Container ships transport goods in standard-size boxes, or containers, which are loaded and unloaded by special gantry cranes. These transfer the containers from and to flattop truck trailers or railroad cars. A similar idea is behind the LASH (lighter aboard ship) system. Goods are packed in standard-sized barges, which are then floated out to a LASH vessel and hauled aboard.

▲ A flotilla of tugs tows out a massive Condeep oil-production platform from the construction site toward the North Sea oil fields. Tugs are the tough workhorses of the oceans. Among their other jobs, they tow barges, help maneuver ocean liners into port, and salvage stricken vessels.

▶ An Iranian supertanker in the Persian Gulf making for a terminal to pick up a cargo of crude oil. Known as VLCCs (very large crude carriers), such vessels can carry hundreds of thousands of tons of oil.

Surface skimmers

Hydroplanes and hydrofoils

Even the fastest ordinary ships cannot travel much faster than about 35 knots, or 65 km/h (40 mph). This is because they expend most of their engine power in overcoming the drag, or resistance, of the water on their hull.

To achieve high speeds, a vessel must somehow raise as much of its hull as possible out of the water. A racing speedboat, or powerboat, achieves this by hydroplaning. As its powerful engine drives it forward, its bow (front) begins to rise out of the water. Most of the rest of its hull follows until only the stern (rear) and the propellers underneath remain submerged. The boat just skims the water.

Hydroplaning is not practical with larger, heavier boats. But they too can skim the surface if they are fitted with underwater "wings." These "wings," called hydrofoils, develop lift when moving through the water in much the same way that aircraft wings (airfoils) develop lift when moving though the air. Hydrofoil boats have two sets of hydrofoils, fore and aft, beneath the hull.

When stationary, and at low speeds, the hull rests in the water, as with an ordinary boat. But as speed increases, the foils start lifting upward. They continue to lift until they raise the hull clear of the water, and only the struts connecting the foils to the hull and the propeller shaft are still in the water. Now almost free from drag, the boat can accelerate to speeds

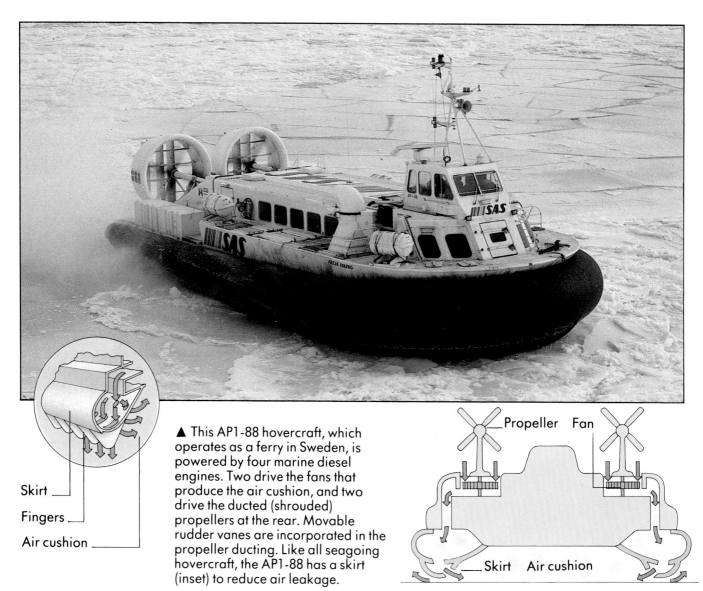

▲ This AP1-88 hovercraft, which operates as a ferry in Sweden, is powered by four marine diesel engines. Two drive the fans that produce the air cushion, and two drive the ducted (shrouded) propellers at the rear. Movable rudder vanes are incorporated in the propeller ducting. Like all seagoing hovercraft, the AP1-88 has a skirt (inset) to reduce air leakage.

Skirt
Fingers
Air cushion

Propeller Fan
Skirt Air cushion

Hydrofoils

Two main kinds of hydrofoils are used on boats. Surface-piercing foils extend out of the water. Fully submerged foils remain beneath the surface. The V-foil surface–piercing type is most widely used but is not suitable for rough waters. The Jetfoil (right) has fully submerged foils.

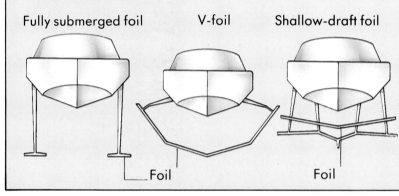

Fully submerged foil   V-foil   Shallow-draft foil

Foil   Foil

as high as 60 knots (110 km/h, or 70 mph).

Hydrofoil vessels are used, particularly in Europe, for swift river transportation and as ferries on short sea crossings. The most sophisticated hydrofoils are the Jetfoils built by the aircraft manufacturer Boeing. They have gas-turbine engines and are notable for being driven by twin water jets.

Hovercraft

On some routes hydrofoil boats have a rival surface skimmer, the hovercraft. This is a kind of air-cushion vehicle, so called because it travels along on a high-pressure bubble, or "cushion" of air. The hovercraft can travel over virtually any surface: solid ground, swamp or water. But it is for water transportation that it has made its mark.

Outstanding are the SRN4 hovercraft ferries that ply the English Channel, which can reach 65 knots (120 km/h, or 75 mph). They have four gas-turbine engines, which drive powerful fans to force air underneath to form a cushion. A flexible "skirt" reduces air leakage. The hull is lifted clear of the water, largely eliminating drag. The engines also drive four large air propellers to provide propulsion. The propellers face backward, operating in a "pushing" mode. Rudders at the rear, in the slipstream of the propellers, provide directional control.

▲ A rear view of an SRN4 hovercraft ferry, showing vehicles unloading and passengers disembarking at a hoverport on the English Channel. The SRN4 is nearly 57 m (190 ft) long and can carry over 400 passengers and 60 cars. The picture shows the "pushing" propellers mounted on pylons, and the twin rudders. Also visible are three engine exhaust nozzles.

◄ The gas-turbine engines of the SRN4 each drive a propeller geared to a fan. The fan sucks in air and forces it through a skirt to create an air cushion.

Submarines and submersibles

Today, the most formidable fighting ships are not surface vessels but nuclear submarines. These craft can lurk undetected in any of the Earth's vast oceans, and can carry enough nuclear missiles to devastate more than a hundred cities.

Submarines submerge by flooding ballast tanks with water, and surface by emptying them using compressed air. Like ordinary ships, they use a propeller for propulsion. It is driven in conventional submarines by a diesel engine on the surface, and by an electric motor underwater. Nuclear submarines are driven by steam turbines. The steam is produced in a generator heated by a compact pressurized-water nuclear reactor.

A submarine is steered through the water by means of a vertical rudder and horizontal fins, called diving planes or hydroplanes. There is one set of planes in the cross-shaped "tail" at the stern, and one on each side near the bow or on the projecting conning tower, or sail. The sail acts as a navigation bridge on the surface. It also houses one or more periscopes and a snorkel tube. The periscopes enable the crew to see above the surface while still remaining submerged. The snorkel enables them to take in air while still submerged.

Nuclear-powered submarines are big; those belonging to the Soviet Union's Typhoon class are 170 m (560 ft.) long and displace 25,000 metric tons. The submarine craft in civilian use, called submersibles, are much smaller. They are now used for ocean research and for supporting offshore oil production. Many are called lockout submersibles. They have a separate diving compartment, which can be pressurized to match the sea.

▶ The U.S. submarine *Will Rogers* is a nuclear-powered, missile-carrying vessel, able to travel underwater for months at a time and go for 600,000 km (nearly 400,000 mi.) or more without refuelling. It has advanced sonar and radar systems. The first nuclear submarine was the USS *Nautilus* in 1954.

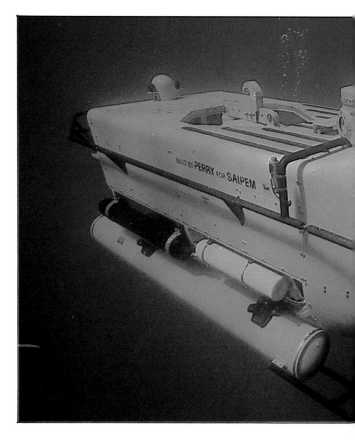

Up and down

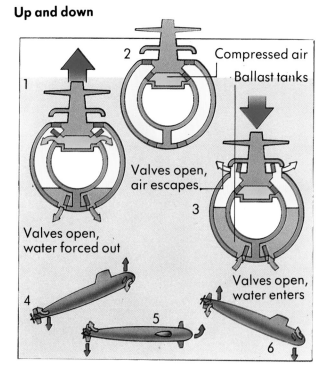

When submerged, the ballast tanks in a submarine contain water. To surface (1), the water is blown out by compressed air. On the surface, the tanks are empty (2). To submerge, water is let into the tanks (3). Moving the diving planes fore and aft puts the nose up (4) or down (6). Moving the rudder achieves sideways control (5).

▲▶ The first submarine, the *Turtle*, invented by the American David Bushnell in 1776 (above), makes an interesting contrast to a modern one-man submersible (right).

◀ This lockout submersible has a hull made of plastic and is powered by an electric motor. In the lockout chamber divers are conditioned for the water pressure outside.

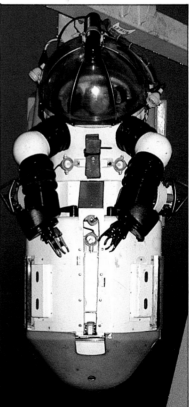

Aircraft

Spot facts

- *The longest airship ever, at 245 m (804 ft.) was the zeppelin* Hindenburg. *It weighed more than 210 metric tons and had a volume of nearly 200,000 cubic meters (over 7 million cu. ft.). It crashed in 1937, killing 36 people.*

- *In June 1979 pilot Bryan Allen pedaled his ultralightweight aircraft* Gossamer Albatross *to make the first human-powered flight across the English Channel. This 2 hour 49 minute flight won a £100,000 (then over $200,000) prize for the aircraft's designer, Paul MacCready.*

- *The Soviet AN-225, the world's biggest aircraft, has a maximum takeoff weight of 600 metric tons. It is 78 m (256 ft.) long, and has a wingspan of 88 m (289 ft.).*

▶ Pedal-powered *Gossamer Albatross* takes to the air. Made of lightweight plastics, it has a 29-m (95-ft.) wingspan and is driven by a single "pushing" propeller. Its cruising speed is 20 km/h (12 mph).

Of all forms of travel on Earth, travel by air is by far the fastest. Ordinary airliners, for example, can carry passengers more than four times as fast as the fastest conventional trains. Aircraft can travel much faster because they are not slowed down by friction as much as vehicles on land and water.

Travel by air began in balloons and airships, but today the skies are dominated by the airplane. The Wright brothers flew the first plane in 1903. It was airborne for only 12 seconds, traveled only about 37 m (120 ft.) and went about as fast as a horse, but it showed the way ahead. Planes today can fly around the world nonstop and travel at many times the speed of sound.

Lighter than air

When a mass of air is heated, it expands. It becomes lighter, or less dense, than the surrounding air. It therefore rises. This simple scientific principle was behind the design of the first aircraft. They were fabric and paper bags containing hot air. Beneath the open neck of the bag a fire was suspended to keep the air warm.

Two French brothers, Joseph and Jacques Montgolfier, launched the first such balloons, making the first major flight at Annonay in June 1783. The hot-air balloon was born. Two months later the noted French physicist J.A.C. Charles launched a quite different design, filling a bag with hydrogen, the lightest of all gases. By the end of 1783 both kinds of balloons were carrying human passengers. Air transport had begun.

In 1852 a French engineer, Henri Giffard, fitted a steam engine to a balloon to create the first dirigible (steerable balloon), or airship. But the airship did not become a practical form of transportation until 1900, when a German Count, Ferdinand von Zeppelin, built the first rigid craft. Like his later designs, it had an aluminum frame covered with fabric. It used bags filled with hydrogen gas to provide lift.

In World War 1 (1914-18) zeppelins carried out the world's first air raids, dropping bombs on London. In 1919 the British airship *R34* made the first two-way crossing of the Atlantic. Ten years later the *Graf Zeppelin* circumnavigated the world in 21 days. It appeared that there was a great future for the airship. But it was not to be. A series of accidents in the 1930s, including the loss of the zeppelin *Hindenburg* in 1937, signaled the end of the airship era.

▲ A modern hot-air balloon. Hot-air ballooning has become a popular sport in recent years. The open fire of the Montgolfier balloon has been replaced by a burner that runs on bottled gas (propane).

◀▲ The German rigid airship *Graf Zeppelin* (left), launched in 1928. Between 1933 and 1937 it operated a transatlantic service between Germany and South America. The modern airship *Europa* (above) is a nonrigid ship, or blimp. It is filled with the nonflammable gas helium, not hydrogen.

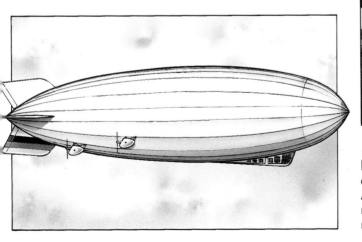

Heavier than air

Every kind of aircraft must lift itself into the air against gravity, and then thrust itself forward against the drag, or resistance, of the air. The thrust may be provided by a propeller or by a jet of hot gases.

The airship is an aircraft that is filled with gas to make it lighter than air. The airplane, the commonest kind of aircraft, is a heavier-than-air machine. It lifts itself into the air by means of its wings, much like a bird does. It uses the principles of aerodynamics, the science of flowing gases.

The wings of a plane have an airfoil shape: broad at the front and sharp at the rear; flat underneath and curved on top. When air moves past an airfoil wing, it travels faster over the upper curved surface than it does under the lower flat one.

As a result, the pressure above the wing becomes lower than the pressure below it. This makes the wing tend to lift upward. And the faster the airflow, the greater the lifting force. When a plane travels fast enough, the lifting force increases until it is greater than the plane's weight, and the plane flies.

▲ The flight deck of an Airbus A310 airliner, showing a bewildering array of instruments.

▼ The action of an airfoil wing produces a pressure difference between top and bottom, which creates lift.

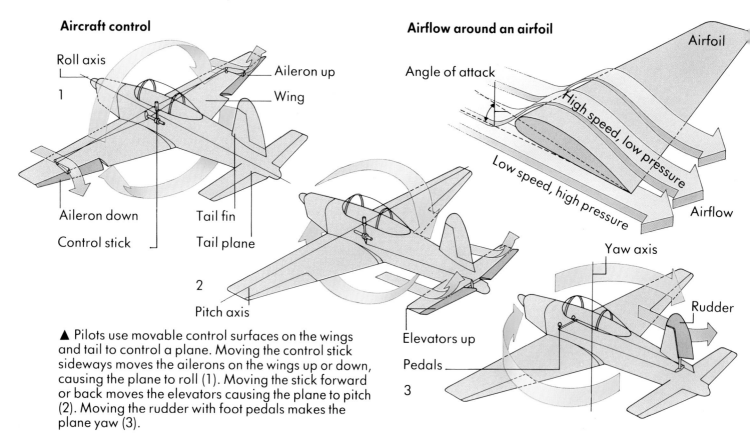

Aircraft control

Roll axis
1
Aileron up
Wing
Aileron down
Control stick
Tail fin
Tail plane
2
Pitch axis

Airflow around an airfoil

Airfoil
Angle of attack
High speed, low pressure
Low speed, high pressure
Airflow

Yaw axis
Rudder
Elevators up
Pedals
3

▲ Pilots use movable control surfaces on the wings and tail to control a plane. Moving the control stick sideways moves the ailerons on the wings up or down, causing the plane to roll (1). Moving the stick forward or back moves the elevators causing the plane to pitch (2). Moving the rudder with foot pedals makes the plane yaw (3).

From *Flyer* to Airbus

The English engineer George Cayley built the first heavier-than-air flying machine, a glider, in 1852. In the 1890s the Wright brothers (U.S.) took up gliding and in 1903 attempted powered flight. On December 17 that year they succeeded, with their *Flyer*, a biplane. In 1909 Louis Blériot (France) crossed the English Channel in a monoplane. Planes like the Sopwith Camel (Great Britain) played a decisive role in World War 1 (1914-18). Speed records began to tumble: in the early 1930s the Supermarine S6B (Great Britain) became the first plane to exceed 400 miles an hour (640 km/h). By the late 1930s scheduled services had begun, operated by planes like the Douglas DC3 Dakota (U.S.). Developments abounded during World War 2 (1939-45), including the first jet plane, the Heinkel He-178 (Germany). Jet airline travel began with the De Havilland Comet (Great Britain) in 1952. In 1969 the first jumbo jet, the Boeing 747 (U.S.), made its maiden flight. A more recent airliner is Europe's "fly-by-wire" Airbus A320.

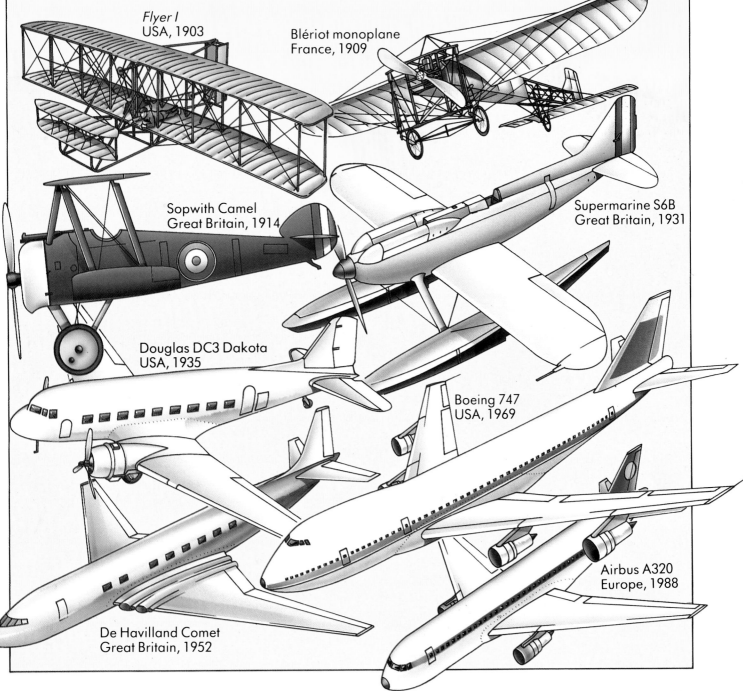

Flyer I
USA, 1903

Blériot monoplane
France, 1909

Sopwith Camel
Great Britain, 1914

Supermarine S6B
Great Britain, 1931

Douglas DC3 Dakota
USA, 1935

Boeing 747
USA, 1969

De Havilland Comet
Great Britain, 1952

Airbus A320
Europe, 1988

Aircraft design

Aircraft of all shapes and sizes fly the air routes of the world. They are differently designed to carry out their different roles. For example, a slow, heavy transport plane like the Super Guppy needs quite a different design from that of an agile, speedy fighter like the F-16.

The Super Guppy has a bulky body. Its wings are long and thick, and stick straight out. It is propeller-driven, with a top speed of below 400 km/h (250 mph). The F-16 by contrast has a sleek, narrow body, with a pointed nose. Its wings are short, thin, and swept back at an angle. It has a top speed of more than 2,000 km/h (1,200 mph).

Long, thick, straight wings are typical of slow

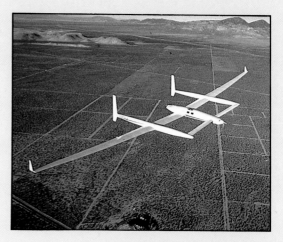

▲ The *Voyager*, in which Dick Rutan and Jeana Yeager circumnavigated the world without refueling on December 14-23, 1986. Its wingspan is 33.8 m (111 ft.).

transport aircraft. Such aircraft use propellers for propulsion, which are efficient at low speeds. These days some propeller aircraft use turboprop engines, in which the propeller is driven by a gas turbine. Additional thrust comes from the jet exhaust. Short, thin, swept-back wings are typical of high-speed aircraft. These use jet engines for propulsion. Fuel burning in the engine produces a stream of hot gases, which shoot backward out of the rear nozzle, and propel the aircraft forward.

The design of airliners lies between these two extremes. They have quite a large fuselage to accommodate passengers and quite thick wings, which are swept back to some extent. Their two, three, or four engines are jets, of a type known as a turbofan. These have a huge

▲ An Airbus A310 airliner of Lufthansa, Germany's national airline. The airliner is built by Airbus Industrie, a French, German, British, and Spanish aerospace consortium. It has a wingspan of nearly 44 m (145 ft.) and a length of nearly 47 m (154 ft.). Its two turbofan engines give it a cruising speed at high altitude of nearly 900 km/h (560 mph).

▲ The Super Guppy, a transport plane with a cavernous body, powered by four turboprop engines. It was designed for NASA in the 1960s to transport parts for the gigantic Saturn V Moon rockets.

▲ Nose view of the Beech Starship 1 plane, which has main wings and "pushing" propellers at the rear.

fan in the intake, which forces air around as well as through the engine and produces a more efficient propulsive jet.

Among the most successful airliners in recent years have been the European Airbus A310 and the wide-bodied U.S. Boeing 747. The Airbus is a two-engined, medium-sized (220-seat) airliner. The Boeing 747, the original jumbo jet, has a larger seating capacity (about 400). It has four engines and a longer operating range: up to 11,000 km (6,800 mi.).

Modern airliners are becoming increasingly expensive. In the early 1990s the 747, for example, cost in the region of $130 million, including spares and crew training. Fewer and fewer companies are able by themselves to finance development and manufacturing costs for new aircraft. This was the reason European companies formed Airbus Industrie.

Supersonic flight

When a plane is flying, it sets up pressure waves in the air. They travel away from the plane at the speed of sound, or sonic speed (Mach 1), which is about 1,200 km/h (750 mph) at sea level. The top speed of most airliners is about 900-950 km/h (560-590 mph). The pressure waves they set up at sonic speed can escape.

However, as a plane's speed approaches that of sound, the pressure waves cannot escape. They bunch up to create shock waves and severe turbulence in the air. This causes buffeting and greatly increased drag on the airframe, and reduces the lift on the wings. The severe forces set up at sonic speed could tear a plane apart. But if it is very carefully designed, it can go supersonic: travel at speeds greater than the speed of sound. It can pass through the "sound barrier" with scarcely a shudder. Indeed, people on the ground underneath are more affected. They hear a noise like a thunderclap as the shock wave passes by. This is called a sonic boom.

Many fighter aircraft are able to accelerate to Mach 2 or 3, or two to three times the speed of sound. These aircraft typically have a pointed nose, a narrow body, and sharply swept-back wings and tail. The Russian Mig-25, or "Foxbat," is an example. Other high-speed planes have wings of triangular shape – the shape of the Greek letter capital delta (Δ).

Planes with sharply swept-back and delta wings, however, have high takeoff and landing speeds and cannot maneuver well at low speeds. This drawback prompted the development of the variable-geometry, or swing-wing design, displayed by the European Tornado and the US F-111. The wings of these planes are movable. For takeoff and low speeds, they extend at right angles to the fuselage, then they swing back for high-speed flight.

Air-traffic control

As more and more planes take to the skies, the work of the air-traffic controllers becomes ever more critical. There are two aspects of control: local, at airports; and regional, along the designated air routes, or "highways" of the air. Both sets of controllers use radio and radar for monitoring and communicating with pilots. They follow the progress of all the planes in their area on radar screens (below).

▲ The distinctive Saab Viggen, designed in Sweden. It is a supersonic interceptor with a double delta wing. The small front wing is called a canard.

▶ The Anglo-French Concorde, the world's only successful supersonic airliner, first flew in 1969. It cruises at Mach 2 at a height of about 16 km (10 mi.).

VTOL craft

A fully-laden Boeing 747 jumbo jet can weigh up to 350 metric tons. During takeoff, it must travel for up to 3 km (nearly 2 mi.) on a prepared runway before its engines have accelerated it to takeoff speed. The need for a long runway for takeoff, and landing too, is a disadvantage with ordinary aircraft. It is a particular drawback for the military, which needs to be able to transport troops and equipment quickly in areas where there may be no runways at all.

It is at such times that it turns to vertical takeoff and landing (VTOL) aircraft. The most common one is the helicopter. A more conventional-looking aircraft with VTOL capability is the Harrier "jump jet."

The helicopter is a nearly perfect flying machine, able to move in any direction in the air and hover like a hummingbird. Whereas airplanes have a fixed wing, helicopters have a rotary wing. This wing provides both the lifting

▼ The fixed-wing Harrier, developed in Great Britain, is a VTOL craft that works by what is called vectored (directional) thrust. Swiveling nozzles direct the jet stream from its engine downward for vertical flight and backward for horizontal flight.

force and the propulsion for flying. The main drawback of the helicopter is its low operating speed, up to only about 300 km/h (less than 200 mph). It cannot travel much faster because otherwise the tips of the rotor blades would approach sonic speed, and the lift on the rotor would fail.

The blades of the helicopter rotor develop lift in much the same way as an ordinary wing, because they have the same airfoil cross section. To fly a helicopter, the pilot alters the amount of lift on the blades and varies the direction of the lift to propel the craft in any direction. He or she uses two main flight controls to achieve this: the collective-pitch lever and the cyclic-pitch stick.

To lift off the ground, the rotor blades are rotated and the pilot increases their pitch – the angle at which they hit the air – by moving the collective-pitch lever. This increases the lift of all the blades equally, and the helicopter takes off vertically. To travel forward, backward or sideways, the pilot operates the cyclic-pitch stick. This varies the pitch of each of the blades so that the resultant lifting force "pulls" the helicopter in the desired direction.

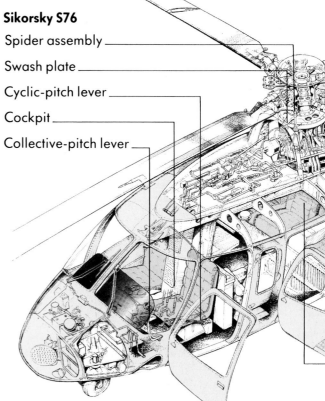

Sikorsky S76

Rotor blades

Spider assembly

Swash plate

Cyclic-pitch lever

Cockpit

Collective-pitch lever

▲ A Boeing Chinook helicopter working in the North Sea oil fields. This 30-seat craft has twin gas-turbine engines and twin rotors turning in opposite directions.

Tail rotor

Tailplane

Turbine exhaust

Tail-rotor drive shaft

Turboshaft engine

Landing gear

Passenger compartment

◀ The Sikorsky S76 has a four-blade main rotor, flexibly hinged at the hub. There is also a rotor spinning vertically at the tail. This is required in single-rotor craft to produce thrust to prevent the helicopter body from spinning as the main rotor spins. This model has two gas-turbine engines, which turn the drive shafts to the rotors. Such engines are termed turboshafts. Linkages in the swash plate and spider assembly alter the pitch of the blades.

▲ A helicopter hovers above a clearing amid a thick canopy of trees in the West African rain forest. It is airlifting equipment being used in seismic surveying for oil. No fixed-wing craft could operate here. Helicopters have a host of commercial uses and are invaluable for sea and mountain rescue work. They can reach places inaccessible by any other means.

Part Two

Travel in space

We and all other living things can exist on Earth only because of the layer of air that surrounds it. This layer, the atmosphere, is thickest at ground level, but gets thinner and thinner the higher up you go. At 200 km (125 mi.) up there is hardly any trace of air, and the atmosphere merges into space.

Space and what is in it have intrigued human beings since the dawn of civilization. But only since the late 1950s have we had the technology to send objects into space to investigate. A few years later, in 1961, human beings began traveling in space.

Since then the space frontier has been pushed far back. Unmanned spacecraft have traveled billions of kilometers to explore other planets and their moons orbiting in the depths of the Solar System. Astronauts have walked on the Moon and have spent over a year in space in Earth-orbiting space stations.

◀ A false-color Landsat image of Abu Dhabi in the Persian Gulf. Satellite imagery of the Earth from space has transformed the work of mapmakers, city planners, and prospectors for oil and minerals.

Into space

Spot facts

- *The world's most powerful rocket, the Soviet Union's Energia, can put into orbit satellites weighing 100 metric tons.*

- *Explorer 1, the first U.S. satellite, circled the Earth 58,376 times during its 12 years in orbit (1958-1970).*

- *The U.S. satellite Lageos, launched in 1976, will not fall back to Earth for 10 million years, when the Earth's surface will have greatly changed.*

- *Some spy satellites, such as the U.S. Big Bird, take photographs that show clearly the letters and figures on car number plates.*

- *After a journey of 7 billion km (over 4 billion mi.), the space probe Voyager 2 was guided in August 1989 to within 5,000 km (nearly 3,000 mi.) of Neptune, then the most distant planet from the Sun in the Solar System.*

▶ Carrying a communications satellite, an Atlas-Centaur rocket blasts off at night from Cape Canaveral in Florida. In a few hours the satellite will be in orbit nearly 36,000 km (over 22,000 mi.) above the Earth's Equator.

High above the Earth in the airless world of space, hundreds of artificial moons, or satellites, circle silently in orbit. Some satellites pick up telephone messages and TV programs from one country and beam them down to others. Some take photographs of the swirling clouds of fierce hurricanes and transmit them back to meteorologists. Others survey the Earth's surface with electronic "eyes" that can reveal otherwise invisible features.

A few spacecraft have escaped from the Earth and are aiming for a distant rendezvous with other planets. Others are heading out of our Solar System and beginning an eons-long voyage to the stars.

Beating gravity

Every piece of matter in the Universe has an attraction for every other piece of matter. This attraction arises from gravitational forces. The English scientist Isaac Newton worked out the basic principles of gravity about 300 years ago. He realized that gravity holds the Universe together. It holds the Earth and the other planets in their paths, or orbits, around the Sun; the Sun and other stars in orbit around the center of our Galaxy; and so on.

On Earth gravity keeps our feet firmly on the ground and holds the gases in the atmosphere. It makes anything we throw up in the air soon come back down again to the ground. The Earth's gravity is very powerful, so how can we beat it and launch objects into space?

Newton worked out how gravity could be beaten by speed. However, to beat gravity an object must be launched from the Earth at the colossal speed of 28,000 km/h (over 17,000 mph). At this speed it will be able to circle around the Earth. Because there is no air in space, there is nothing to slow the object down. It will continue circling at the same speed, in orbit, as an artificial Earth satellite.

▶ A cross section of the Earth's atmosphere. The air is thickest at the bottom. It thins out with increasing height until it merges into space. But faint traces of air remain even as high as 200 km (125 mi.).

▼ Isaac Newton drew this diagram to show how to beat gravity. If you throw a ball faster and faster, it will travel farther and farther before falling back to Earth. At a very high speed indeed, the ball will "fall around the Earth" and enter orbit.

Into orbit

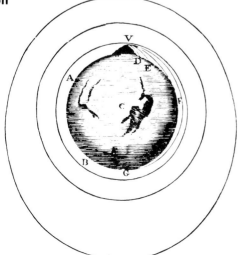

Earth's atmosphere

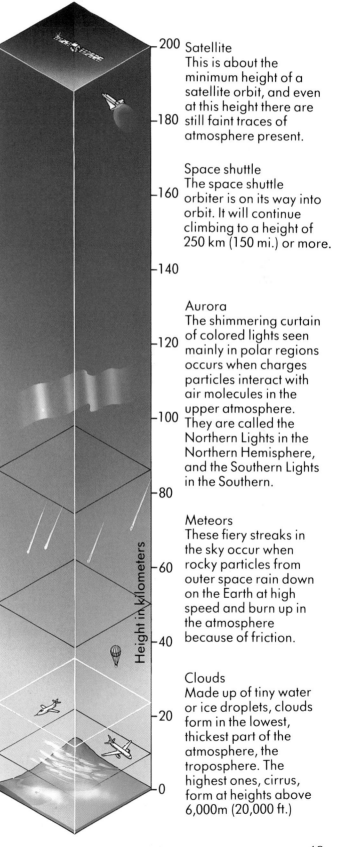

Satellite
This is about the minimum height of a satellite orbit, and even at this height there are still faint traces of atmosphere present.

Space shuttle
The space shuttle orbiter is on its way into orbit. It will continue climbing to a height of 250 km (150 mi.) or more.

Aurora
The shimmering curtain of colored lights seen mainly in polar regions occurs when charges particles interact with air molecules in the upper atmosphere. They are called the Northern Lights in the Northern Hemisphere, and the Southern Lights in the Southern.

Meteors
These fiery streaks in the sky occur when rocky particles from outer space rain down on the Earth at high speed and burn up in the atmosphere because of friction.

Clouds
Made up of tiny water or ice droplets, clouds form in the lowest, thickest part of the atmosphere, the troposphere. The highest ones, cirrus, form at heights above 6,000m (20,000 ft.)

Communications, weather satellites

Perhaps the most useful kinds of satellites are those that relay, or pass on, communications between distant areas. These communications satellites handle all kinds of electronic communications in the form of microwaves, or very short radio waves, including telephone calls, radio broadcasts and TV programs.

Signals are beamed up to the satellites and received back from them by huge dish antennas at ground stations. These are linked into the local communications systems by cable or microwave radio links.

Intelsat (International Telecommunications Satellite Organization) is the biggest worldwide satellite communications network. It has over 110 member nations, and operates powerful communications satellites, such as *Intelsat 6*, over the Atlantic, Pacific, and Indian Oceans. The satellites are in geostationary orbit: they circle over the Equator at a height of 35,900 km (22,300 mi.). In this orbit they circle the Earth every 24 hours. They keep pace with the Earth as it turns, and appear fixed in the sky.

The Soviet Union maintains a fairly large communications satellite network known as

The first Sputnik

The Soviet Union thrust the world into the Space Age on October 4, 1957, when it launched *Sputnik 1* with a modified Sapwood intercontinental ballistic missile (ICBM). It was an aluminum sphere measuring 58 cm (1.9 ft.) across and weighing 84 kg (184 lb.). It sent back simple radio signals from its four long antennas. Its orbit took it as low as 227 km (141 mi.) above the Earth, and the whiff of atmosphere there gradually caused it to slow down.

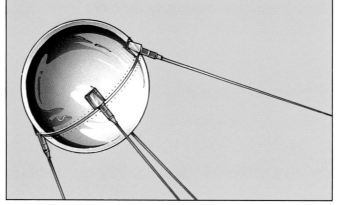

◀ A satellite dish in a remote village in India. It receives signals from a communications satellite in geostationary orbit, 35,900 km (22,300 mi.) high. The satellite beams down regular television programs for entertainment and also specialist programs for education and instruction in, for example, farming and family health.

▼ A GOES weather satellite and an image taken by *GOES 4* in geostationary orbit over the eastern Atlantic Ocean. It shows a hurricane (David), spiraling over the Caribbean islands of Hispaniola and Puerto Rico. The central core of the hurricane measures more than 400 km (250 mi.) across.

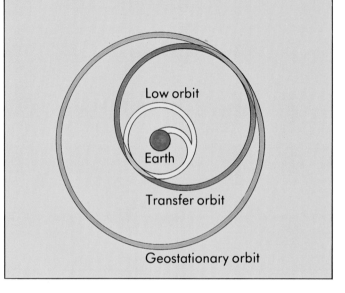

Geostationary orbit

Most satellites that need to reach geostationary orbit 35,900 km (22,300 mi.) high are first launched into low orbit. Then their on-board motor fires to send them into a transfer orbit. When they are 35,900 km high, the motor fires again to direct them into a circular geostationary orbit.

Low orbit

Earth

Transfer orbit

Geostationary orbit

Orbita, which uses Molniya satellites. They do not circle in geostationary orbits, but in orbits that are eccentric, or highly elliptical. These orbits take them as high as 40,000 km (25,000 mi.) over the Soviet Union but as low as 600 km (370 mi.) on the other side of the Earth. In this way they are "in sight" of Soviet ground stations for most of the time.

Weather forecasting has been revolutionized by the use of satellites. They are able to scan the whole Earth and the atmosphere continuously. They can show how weather systems are developing anywhere in the world, even where there are no ground weather stations. They take cloud pictures, measure water and air temperature, and relay weather data.

Some weather satellites circle in geostationary orbit, where they view nearly a whole hemisphere. The U.S. GOES and European Meteosat satellites are examples. Other satellites, such as the U.S. NOAA series, are launched into a polar orbit, over the North and South Poles. They can scan the whole Earth every 12 hours as it spins beneath them.

Earth-survey satellites

Mapmakers, city planners, mineral prospectors, farmers, and foresters are among the many groups of people who have benefited from another kind of satellite. This is the Earth-survey, or Earth-resources satellite.

At the beginning of the Space Age, ordinary photographs of the Earth's surface from orbit revealed much useful information. Earth-survey satellites are able to gather even more by scanning the surface in light of different wavelengths, such as infrared.

The best-known series of such satellites has been the U.S. Landsats, of which five were launched between 1972 and 1984. *Landsat 5* orbits at an altitude of about 700 km (435 mi.). Using an oscillating-mirror system, it scans the Earth's surface in 185-km (115-mi.) square blocks in green and red visible light and at four infrared wavelengths.

The French SPOT satellites and the European Space Agency's *ERS-1* are also Earth-survey satellites. *ERS-1* uses scanning radar and also monitors weather and climate.

Information comes back from the satellites in the form of electronic data. Computers process the data and display it as images. They can manipulate the data in various ways and display it in false-color pictures. The colors are chosen so as to pick out certain features of the landscape. This is possible because every kind of feature has a different "spectral signature". This means that it reflects different wavelengths in its own particular way.

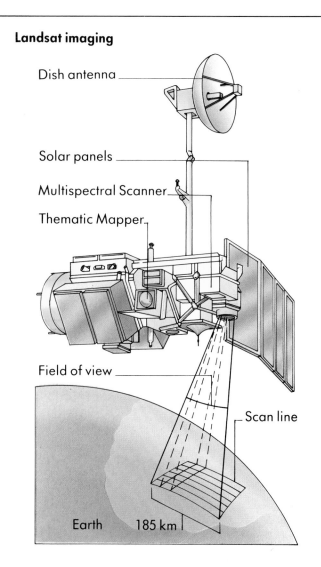

Landsat imaging

Dish antenna

Solar panels

Multispectral Scanner

Thematic Mapper

Field of view

Scan line

Earth   185 km

The *Landsat 5* satellite (top) pictures the Earth using two scanning systems, the Thematic Mapper and the Multispectral Scanner. Both scan the Earth in 185-km (115-mi.) swathes at several wavelengths. The received data can be displayed in false colors on screen (above) or on film (opposite) in a number of different ways.

SPOT 1

The French Earth-resources satellite *SPOT* (Satellite Probatoire pour l'Observation de la Terre) has better resolution than Landsat. It can spot details as small as 10 m (roughly 30 ft.) – about the size of a bus. Like Landsat, it scans at different wavelengths.

Probes to other worlds

If you launch a spacecraft with a speed of 28,000 km/h (over 17,000 mph), it will go into orbit as a satellite. But it is still tied to Earth by gravity. You have to launch a spacecraft with a much higher speed if you want it to escape from the Earth's gravity completely. This speed, called escape velocity, is no less than 40,000 km/h (25,000 mph). This is nearly 20 times the speed of the supersonic airliner Concorde.

A spacecraft that escapes from the Earth is called a space probe. The first probes were sent to the Moon. The Soviet Union first achieved success in 1959, when its probe *Luna 2* crash-landed there. Later, Soviet and U.S. lunar probes went into orbit around the Moon and landed on it. Exploration of the planets from space began in 1962, when the U.S. probe *Mariner 2* flew close (35,000 km, or 22,000 mi.) to Venus. Since then probes have visited all the planets in our Solar System except Pluto. They have also flown to meet Halley's comet.

Targeting the planets
There are all kinds of problems involved in sending probes to the planets. One is distance. Even our nearest planetary neighbor, Venus, never comes closer to us than 42 million km (26 million mi.). And the most distant planet from the Sun at the moment, Neptune, lies more than 4 billion km (2.5 billion mi.). Using the rockets we have at present, it takes a probe several months to reach even Venus and Mars. It takes years to reach the more distant planets: Jupiter, Saturn, Uranus, and so on.

Another problem is aiming the probe. It must be aimed at a point in space in the target planet's orbit so that it will arrive at the same time as the planet. If the probe leaves the Earth in slightly the wrong direction or at slightly the wrong speed, then it could miss its target by hundreds of thousands of kilometers.

Keeping in touch
Maintaining communications with a probe over many millions of kilometers is also a major problem. The probe must be tracked precisely so

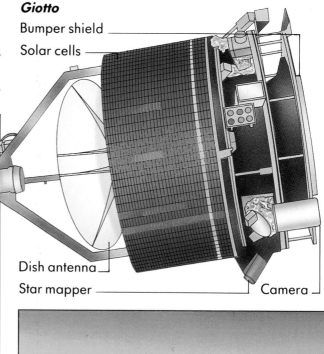

Giotto
Bumper shield
Solar cells
Dish antenna
Star mapper
Camera

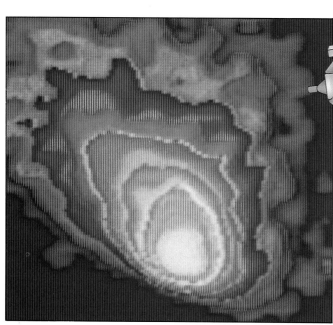

▲ A false-color image of Halley's comet, from data returned by the European space probe *Giotto* in March 1986. At the time the probe was less than 1,000 km (600 mi.) away. It took a beating from the rocky debris around the comet, but managed to survive.

that radio signals can be beamed in the right direction in space. To send and receive signals, large dish antennas are used. NASA, the National Aeronautics and Space Administration of the United States, communicates with U.S. space probes through its Deep Space Network. This comprises tracking stations at Goldstone in California, at Madrid in Spain, and at Canberra in Australia. They use dish antennas up to 70 m (230 ft.) across.

Because the probes are so far away, there is a time lag between the sending and receiving of signals between the tracking station and the probes. When *Voyager 2* sent radio signals back from Neptune in 1989, they took over four hours to reach the Earth. The transmitter on the probe has a power output about the same as the bulb in a refrigerator. Yet NASA scientists were able to convert the signals into remarkably clear pictures.

Viking

Dish antenna
Meteorology sensors
Seismometer
Roll engines
UHF antenna

Biology processor

Cameras

Footpad
Descent engine

Digging arm

Collector head

Pioneer 11

Magnetometer

RTGs

Imaging system

Dish antenna

Cosmic-ray telescope

Particle detector

Meteoroid-detector panel

Thrusters

Radioisotope thermoelectric generators (RTGs)

▲ *Pioneer 10* and its twin, *Pioneer 11*, were the first probes to journey through the asteroid belt to the giant planet Jupiter, in 1973 and 1974, respectively. In addition, *Pioneer 11* continued on to Saturn, which it reached in 1979. Because they traveled so far from the Sun, the Pioneers carried nuclear batteries (RTGs) to power their instruments.

◄ Two Viking probes landed on Mars in 1976, and took close-up pictures of its surface (photo). The pictures revealed that the surface is rust-red in color, and even the sky has a reddish tinge. Automatic soil samplers tested for signs of life, but in vain. The probes reported average temperatures up to −30°C (−22°F) and winds gusting up to 120 km/h (75 mph).

Voyager 2

The US spacecraft *Voyager 2* has been the most successful probe ever launched. It began its journey of discovery in 1977, reaching Jupiter in 1979, Saturn in 1981, Uranus in 1986, and Neptune in 1989. And what sights it saw: raging storms on Jupiter, sulfur volcanoes on Jupiter's moon Io; tiny "shepherd" moons of Saturn that keep its rings in place; crazy landscapes on Uranus's moon Miranda; and geysers of liquid gas on Neptune's moon Triton.

Voyager 2's "grand tour" of the outer planets was made possible by two things. The planets were aligned in space in a favorable way. This happens only once every 175 years. Also, *Voyager 2* used the assistance of gravity to direct and accelerate it from planet to planet.

The gravity-assist technique was first used with *Mariner 10*, launched in 1973, to enable the probe to visit both Venus and Mercury. On a gravity-assist mission, a probe is targeted close to a planet. The planet's gravity then makes the probe speed up and curve around the planet before being slung in another direction.

Voyager 2 is now heading out of our Solar System toward interstellar space. It set out from Earth about two weeks before its sister craft *Voyager 1*. *Voyager 1* visited only Jupiter and Saturn before heading for the stars.

It is just possible, in eons to come, that the Voyagers might be found by intelligent beings from another planet in another solar system. In case they are, they both carry phonograph records called "Sounds of Earth". On these are recorded greetings from Earth people in 60 languages, sounds from nature and the human world, and, in code, a selection of photographs. Helpfully, instructions on how to play the disks are given in pictorial form on the record covers.

▶ The path *Voyager 2* took through the Solar System on a 12-year, four-planet mission of discovery that cannot be repeated for more than a century and a half. *Voyager 2* set out from Earth on August 20, 1977. It arrived at its last port of call, Neptune, on August 25, 1989. Its journey of 7 billion km (over 4 billion mi.) had been so well planned that it was able to swoop to within 5,000 km (nearly 3,000 mi.) of Neptune's cloud tops. Now it is heading toward the heliopause, the boundary between the Solar System and interstellar space. In 300,000 years' time it should pass within a few light-years of Sirius, the brightest star.

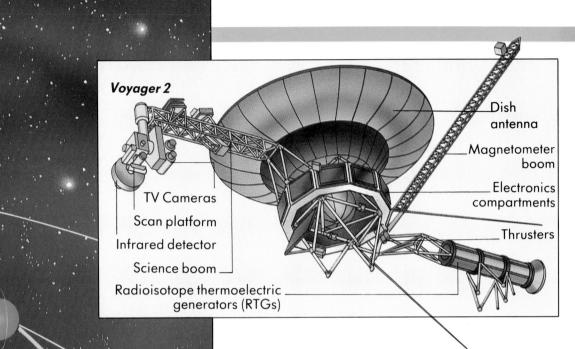

Voyager 2

TV Cameras
Scan platform
Infrared detector
Science boom
Radioisotope thermoelectric generators (RTGs)

Dish antenna
Magnetometer boom
Electronics compartments
Thrusters

▲ *Voyager 2* uses a 3.7-m (12-ft.) dish antenna to transmit radio signals back to Earth. A boom 12m (40 ft.) long carries the magnetometers. The scan platform carries most of the other instruments, including particle and radiation detectors and two TV cameras.

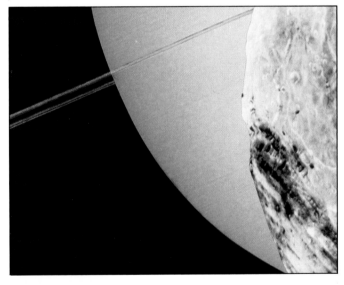

8

10

7

1 Sun
2 Mercury
3 Venus
4 Earth
5 Mars
6 Jupiter
7 Saturn
8 Uranus
9 Neptune
10 Asteroids

***Voyager 2* images**

Voyager 2 sent back tens of thousands of images during its remarkable mission. It spied the multicolored disk of giant Jupiter (far left), Saturn's glorious rings, and several of Saturn's moons (left). At Uranus, *Voyager 2* spotted a system of faint rings (above), seen here looking across the rugged surface of the moon Miranda. Neptune (top left) was revealed as a blue cloud-flecked planet with dark spots, which are probably huge storms.

Space transportation

Engineers in the Soviet Union and the United States began designing suitable vehicles for transporting human beings into space almost as soon as the Space Age began in 1957. But the first manned spacecraft, such as Vostok, Mercury, and Gemini, were cramped, uncomfortable capsules. The next-generation Apollo and Soyuz spacecraft had only marginally more room. But the Apollo craft nevertheless supported crews of three astronauts on daring flights to the Moon and back, not once but nine times. Not until 1981 did the modern era of space travel begin, at least for Americans, using the space shuttle, the world's first reusable spaceship. The Soviets launched a shuttle craft in 1988.

▶ Astronaut Eugene Cernan takes the lunar roving vehicle for a test drive during the Apollo 17 Moon-landing mission in December 1972. The collapsible "Moon buggy" was powered by electric motors and had a top speed of 16 km/h (10 mph).

Early days

A Soviet Air Force major, Yuri Gagarin, made the first human flight in space on April 12, 1961. He orbited the Earth once in a *Vostok 1* capsule, landing by parachute after ejecting. Cosmonaut Gagarin was aloft for 108 minutes.

The United States, racing to catch up, managed to launch Alan Shepard in a Mercury capsule named *Freedom 7* on a 15-minute suborbital flight into space on May 5, 1961. Not until February 20, 1962, did John Glenn become the first American in orbit, circling the Earth three times in the Mercury capsule *Friendship 7*. They both splashed down at sea.

The Soviets launched the first multiple crew into space in a modified Vostok craft called *Voskhod 1* in October 1964. The second-generation U.S. spacecraft was the Gemini. It was named after the constellation of the zodiac whose English name is the Twins. It was an apt name because the Gemini craft carried a crew of two. Ten highly successful manned Gemini flights took place in 1965 and 1966, during which the astronauts practiced spacewalking, maneuvering in orbit, and other techniques that would be needed on the Apollo missions.

▲ Virgil Grissom in the Mercury capsule *Liberty Bell 7* blasts off the pad at Cape Canaveral, Florida, on July 21, 1961 to begin a 15-minute suborbital flight.

Pioneering spacecraft

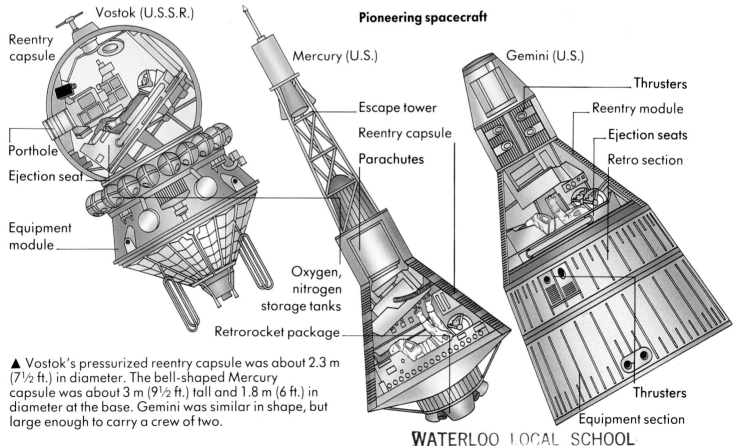

Vostok (U.S.S.R.)
Reentry capsule
Porthole
Ejection seat
Equipment module

Mercury (U.S.)
Escape tower
Reentry capsule
Parachutes
Oxygen, nitrogen storage tanks
Retrorocket package

Gemini (U.S.)
Thrusters
Reentry module
Ejection seats
Retro section
Thrusters
Equipment section

▲ Vostok's pressurized reentry capsule was about 2.3 m (7½ ft.) in diameter. The bell-shaped Mercury capsule was about 3 m (9½ ft.) tall and 1.8 m (6 ft.) in diameter at the base. Gemini was similar in shape, but large enough to carry a crew of two.

Apollo

On May 25, 1961 the U.S. President John F. Kennedy urged the American people to undertake the greatest adventure in the history of humankind. "I believe that this nation should commit itself," he said, "to achieving the goal, before this decade is out, of landing a man on the Moon and returning him safely to Earth."

This plea gave birth to the Apollo Moon-landing project. The United States actually achieved not just one, but two landings before the decade was out. The first landing, on July 20, 1969, saw *Apollo 11* astronauts Neil Armstrong and Edwin Aldrin walking on the Moon's Sea of Tranquillity. They were followed over the next three-and-a-half years by five more crews, from *Apollo 12, 14, 15, 16* and *17*. *Apollo 13* aimed for a Moon landing but was nearly blasted apart on the way. The crew just managed to make it safely back to Earth. The *Apollo 17* astronauts left the Moon on December 14, 1972.

To launch human beings to the Moon and bring them back safely was an enormous undertaking. It required a great technological effort and also the creation of some gigantic

Main engine nozzle

▲ A Saturn V rocket thunders away from the launchpad on December 21, 1968, carrying three astronauts in *Apollo 8* to the first human encounter of the Moon.

To the Moon and back

The technique Apollo used to reach the Moon was called lunar orbit rendezvous. The Apollo spacecraft lifted off atop a Saturn V rocket (1,2,3). It was then accelerated out of Earth orbit (4) and configured for the outward journey (5,6,7). Retrofire (8) took it into lunar orbit, where the lunar module (LM) separated (9) and landed (10). After the landing mission, the top part of the LM took off (11) and rendezvoused with the mother ship (12). A burn of the main engine (13) boosted the craft out of lunar orbit for the return to Earth. Before reentry the service module was jettisoned (14). The command module, traveling at nearly 11 km (7 mi.) a second and with heat shield reddening (15), plunged through the atmosphere. The air slowed it down, then parachutes opened to lower it to a gentle splashdown (16).

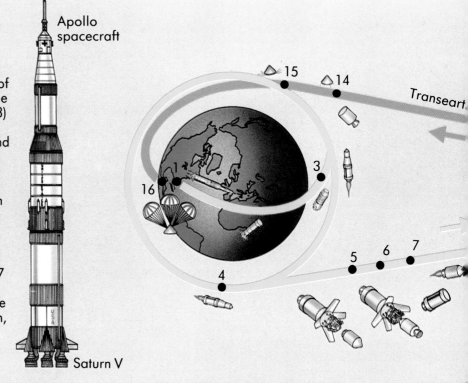

Apollo spacecraft

Saturn V

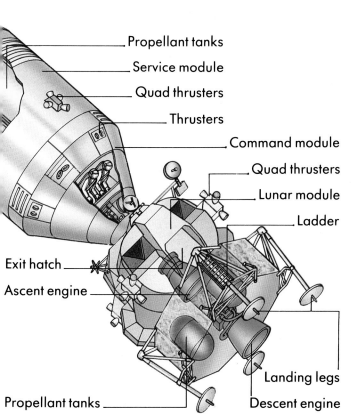

Apollo spacecraft

Propellant tanks
Service module
Quad thrusters
Thrusters
Command module
Quad thrusters
Lunar module
Ladder
Exit hatch
Ascent engine
Propellant tanks
Landing legs
Descent engine

structures and equipment. To launch the 45-metric ton Apollo spacecraft required a mammoth rocket, the Saturn V, which stood 111 m (364 ft.) high and weighed 3,000 metric tons.

To assemble such a giant required a massive building, the Vehicle Assembly Building, at the launch site, the Kennedy Space Center in Florida. This building, now used to assemble the space shuttle, measures 160 m (525 ft.) high, 158 m (518 ft.) wide and 218 m (715 ft.) long.

A three-module design was adopted to fit in with the technique chosen for the Moon landing, called lunar orbit rendezvous. The main part of the craft was the pressurized command module (CM), which housed the crew of three. This was the only part to return to Earth. For most of the mission it was attached to the service module (SM), the combined unit being termed the CSM. The third unit was the lunar module (LM), the spacecraft used to ferry two of the crew to and from the Moon's surface.

◄ The three modules of the Apollo spacecraft, linked together for the journey to the Moon. It was about 17 m (56 ft.) long overall and up to about 4 m (13 ft.) across. It had an Earth weight of about 45 metric tons.

▼ On the *Apollo 15* mission James Irwin is pictured with the lunar module and lunar roving vehicle. Behind him are the Apennine Mountains.

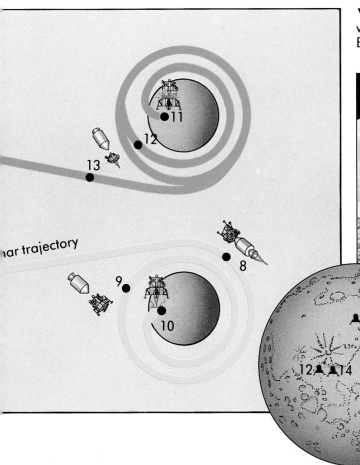

ar trajectory

◄ Sites of the six Apollo landings. *Apollo 11* landed on the Sea of Tranquillity; *Apollo 12* on the Ocean of Storms; *Apollo 14* near the Fra Mauro crater; *Apollo 15* and *17* on the edge of the Sea of Serenity; and *Apollo 16* on the Descartes plateau.

Soyuz

Soviet space scientists developed a successor to their Vostok and Voskhod spacecraft at much the same time as the United States developed Apollo. The Soviet craft, called Soyuz, made its maiden flight in April 1967. But it ended in tragedy when its pilot, cosmonaut Vladimir Komarov, was killed during landing. He was the first known in-flight casualty of the Space Age. Even today Soviet cosmonauts make their journeys into space in a version of the Soyuz spacecraft. The Soviet shuttle craft, called *Buran*, may eventually be used as a ferry.

Soyuz, like Apollo, is made up of three modules. It measures nearly 8 m (26 ft.) long and up to 2.7 m (10 ft.) across. At the front is the orbital module, in which the crew can work in orbit. It has a hatch by which the craft can link up, or dock, with Soviet space stations. The crew usually occupies the center section, the command and reentry module. At the rear is the instrument module, which contains equipment, fuel, and rocket motors. The front and rear modules separate before reentry. The reentry module is braked first by the atmosphere, then by parachutes, and finally, just before landing,

▲ The Apollo spacecraft, with docking module attached, pictured in orbit during the ASTP mission in July 1975. The picture was taken from the Soyuz spacecraft.

Docking target

Docking module

Apollo spacecraft

Oxygen bottle

Nitrogen bottle

▲ This artist's impression records the historic moment on July 17, 1975, when U.S. astronauts in Apollo (bottom) and Soviet cosmonauts in Soyuz met and shook hands in orbit on the ASTP mission. The two craft remained docked together for 47 hours. The U.S. crew members were Thomas Stafford, Vance Brand, and Donald Slayton. The Soviet crew were Aleksei Leonov and Valery Kubasov. In 1965 Leonov had made the first spacewalk.

Command module

Handshake in orbit

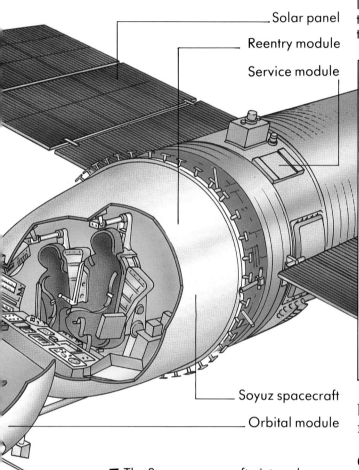

Solar panel

Reentry module

Service module

Soyuz spacecraft

Orbital module

▼ The Soyuz spacecraft pictured from Apollo during the ASTP mission. At the front of the craft (left), on the spherical orbital module, is the docking mechanism.

▼ A Soyuz spacecraft and launch vehicle on the launchpad at the Baikonur Cosmodrome in Central Asia. The gantry structure is being retracted prior to a launch. On the pad the vehicle stands 45 m (150 ft.) tall. Unlike U.S. rockets, Soviet launch vehicles are put together horizontally and then tilted upright on the pad.

by retrorockets. The crew stays inside the module all the way down.

Cooperation in the cosmos

At the beginning of the Space Age the Soviet Union and the United States were battling with each other for supremacy in space. This became known as the Space Race. In 1975, however, old rivalries were set aside, at least temporarily, when the two space powers mounted a joint mission, the Apollo-Soyuz Test Project (ASTP).

To allow the two craft to dock together, a special docking module was designed. It had two docking ports: one fitted the Apollo, and the other the Soyuz docking systems. Apollo flew into orbit with the docking module attached on July 15, 1975, from the Kennedy Space Center in Florida. Soyuz had been launched a few hours before from its usual launch site, the Baikonur Cosmodrome in Central Asia. On July 17, the two craft met up and docked with each other. They remained docked for nearly two days, while the astronauts dined, relaxed, and carried out a number of experiments together.

The shuttle system

All of the rocket launch vehicles used in the first two decades of space flight were expendable. This means that they could be used only once. This represented a very wasteful kind of technology. It made more sense, surely, to design a vehicle that could be used again and again. This thinking led to the birth of the U.S. space shuttle, which made its maiden flight into orbit in 1981.

Three main elements make up the space shuttle transportation system. The main one is the winged orbiter, which carries the crew and the payload (cargo). It rides into space on top of a huge external tank, which carries fuel for its engines. Strapped to the sides of the tank are twin solid rocket boosters.

These elements are put together in the cavernous Vehicle Assembly Building at Complex 39 at the Kennedy Space Center in Florida, the main shuttle launch site. They are mounted

▼ On April 12, 1981, orbiter *Columbia* soars from the launchpad on the first space shuttle mission. On board are test pilots John Young and Robert Crippen. They touch down 54 hours later at the Edwards Air Force Base in California after a flawless flight.

▼ The space shuttle orbiter is launched like a rocket, acts like a spacecraft in space, and lands on a runway like an aircraft. It is blasted from the pad by its three main engines and twin solid rocket boosters (SRBs), which together develop a thrust of more than 3,300,000 kg (7.2 million lb.). On its way into orbit, it sheds its boosters and external tank in turn. To return to Earth, the orbiter fires retrorockets and drops from orbit. Friction with the air slows it down and makes its heat shield redden. It makes an unpowered runway landing, like a glider, and is later flown back by jumbo jet to its launch site.

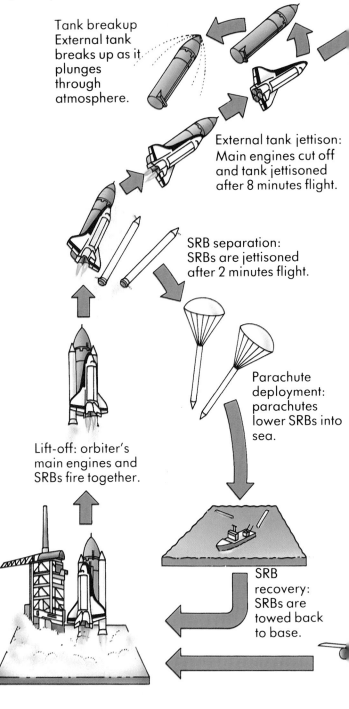

Tank breakup
External tank breaks up as it plunges through atmosphere.

External tank jettison: Main engines cut off and tank jettisoned after 8 minutes flight.

SRB separation: SRBs are jettisoned after 2 minutes flight.

Parachute deployment: parachutes lower SRBs into sea.

SRB recovery: SRBs are towed back to base.

Lift-off: orbiter's main engines and SRBs fire together.

From lift-off to landing

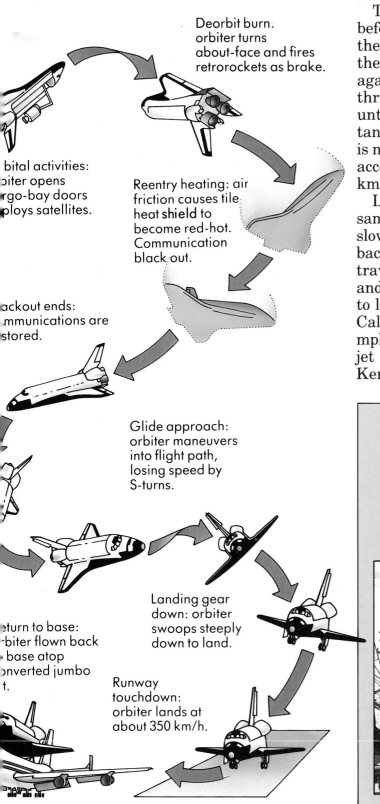

Deorbit burn. orbiter turns about-face and fires retrorockets as brake.

bital activities: iter opens rgo-bay doors ploys satellites.

Reentry heating: air friction causes tile heat **shield** to become red-hot. Communication black out.

ackout ends: mmunications are stored.

Glide approach: orbiter maneuvers into flight path, losing speed by S-turns.

Landing gear down: orbiter swoops steeply down to land.

turn to base: biter flown back base atop nverted jumbo t.

Runway touchdown: orbiter lands at about 350 km/h.

vertically on a mobile launch platform, which is carried out to the launchpad by a huge crawler transporter.

The solid rocket boosters fire for two minutes before falling away. They parachute down to the ocean, where they are recovered. They are then towed back to the Space Center to be used again. The main engines meanwhile continue to thrust the shuttle ever faster, ever higher, until, after eight minutes of flight, the external tank runs out of fuel. This is then discarded, and is not recovered. Two small engines then fire to accelerate the orbiter to orbital velocity (28,000 km/h, or over 17,000 mph) and place it in orbit.

Later, at the end of the shuttle mission, these same engines fire again as retrorockets. They slow down the orbiter so that gravity can pull it back to Earth. It reenters the atmosphere traveling at about 25 times the speed of sound, and air friction rapidly slows it down. It glides in to land, usually at Edwards Air Force Base in California, at a speed of about 350 km/h (220 mph). A specially converted Boeing 747 carrier jet is on hand to transport it back to the Kennedy launch site, for its next mission.

Russia's shuttle

On November 15, 1988, a Soviet space shuttle lifted off from Baikonur Cosmodrome in Central Asia. The winged orbiter, named *Buran*, was making its maiden, unmanned flight. *Buran* looks much like the U.S. shuttle orbiter. It rides into space on the world's most powerful launch vehicle, Energia.

Shuttle hardware

The orbiter is the key part of the space shuttle system. It is ingeniously designed to be part rocket, part spacecraft, and part aircraft, and it performs all these functions well. A fleet of four orbiters was originally planned: *Columbia*, *Challenger*, *Discovery*, and *Atlantis*.

On making its second flight into orbit in November 1981, *Columbia* became the first launch vehicle ever to return to space. *Challenger* met a tragic end on its tenth flight in January 1986, when it exploded 73 seconds after lift-off, killing its crew of seven. Shuttle operations were suspended until September 1988 to allow modifications of the hardware and of management procedures to take place. Construction of a replacement orbiter, *Endeavor*, proceeded.

The crew of up to eight people rides in the forward fuselage of the orbiter, pressurized with air at normal pressure. Two astronauts fly the craft from a cockpit at the front of the upper, or flight, deck. The cockpit looks much like that of a modern airliner, but has more switches, instruments, and controls. It also incorporates video display units connecting with the orbiter's powerful computer system.

The orbiter carries its payload in the huge cargo bay, which measures 18 m (60 ft.) long and 4.5 m (15 ft.) across. Because it is so large, the bay can accommodate two or more satellites

Space shuttle construction

Remote manipulator system
Getaway Specials
Cargo bay
Satellite pods
Rudder

OMS engine
OMS/RCS propellants
Main engines

Body flap
RCS thrusters
Separation motors
SRB (solid rocket booster)

Delta wing
Elevons

▶ The delta-winged space shuttle orbiter is about the size of a medium-sized airliner, with a length of 37 m (122 ft.) and a wingspan of nearly 24 m (78 ft.). On the launch pad it weighs about 90 metric tons. The biggest part of the shuttle system is the external tank, which measures 47 m (154 ft.) long. It holds some 2 million liters (500,000 gallons) of liquid hydrogen and liquid oxygen, the propellants for the orbiter's three main engines. Strapped to the tank are two boosters, which burn solid propellants. The solid rocket boosters (SRBs) are 45.5 m (over 149 ft.) long and nearly 4 m in diameter. They are made up of thick steel segments, locked together by pins. The joints are sealed by sets of rings.

◄ A close-up of the instrument panel in the cockpit of the space shuttle orbiter, showing the cathode-ray tube displays. They are tied into the powerful computer system that operates the orbiter. The pilot and commander can call up all kinds of data on the screens via computer keyboards.

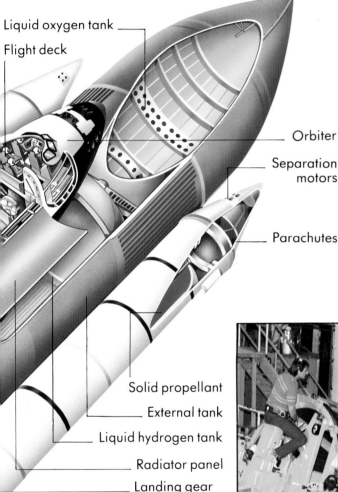

Liquid oxygen tank
Flight deck

Orbiter

Separation motors

Parachutes

Solid propellant
External tank
Liquid hydrogen tank
Radiator panel
Landing gear
Carbon insulation

► A replacement main engine being maneuvered into position in the tail section of the orbiter *Discovery* in preparation for space shuttle mission STS-26. The mission, which eventually took place in September 1988, was the first since *Challenger* exploded in the Florida skies just after lift-off on January 28, 1986. That tragedy, in which seven astronauts died, forced a complete rethinking of shuttle design and operational procedures to ensure greater safety in the future.

at the same time. On some missions it carries a single large payload, such as the European-built Spacelab, a fully equipped scientific laboratory. Around the major payloads, the bay also has room for so-called Getaway Specials. These are experiments by small research teams that can "hitch a ride" into space at low cost.

The tail section houses the three main engines and the two engines of the orbital maneuvering system (OMS). The OMS engines fire to inject the orbiter into orbit and to brake the craft prior to reentry. The tail section also carries sets of thrusters for the reaction control system (RCS), by which the pilots can change the position, or attitude, of the craft in space.

To prevent the aluminum airframe of the orbiter from overheating when reentering the atmosphere, it is covered with insulation. Much of the orbiter is covered with a layer of ceramic tiles made of silica. Over 30,000 tiles are required, each one individually tailored for a particular location. On the nose and wing edges, where temperature can soar to over 1,500°C (2,700°F), a carbon refractory material is used.

Shuttle operations

On most shuttle missions the main objective is to launch satellites. Launch operations are carried out from a control panel at the rear of the orbiter flight deck. From there astronauts can look through windows into the cargo bay.

Satellites may be launched in a number of ways. They can be sprung out of a pod or rolled from the bay rather like a Frisbee. They can also be literally placed in orbit by the shuttle's "crane," the robot arm of the remote manipulator system. The Hubble Space Telescope, for example, was launched in this manner in 1990. The robot arm, which is 15 m (50 ft.) long, extends from inside the payload bay. It has flexible joints and a snare device at the "hand" end to grip the satellites.

The shuttle usually goes into orbit at a height of 250-320 km (150-200 mi.) or so. This is much too low for many of the satellites it launches. Most communications satellites, for example, need to orbit at 35,900 km (22,300 mi.). So these satellites have a booster rocket attached, which fires to lift them to high orbit. Shuttle-launched probes destined to explore the planets likewise carry a powerful booster to accelerate them to escape velocity.

The robot arm is also put to good use in retrieving satellites from orbit. This technique was first used in 1984 to capture a satellite called *Solar Max*, which had malfunctioned only a few months after launch four years before. After the satellite had been captured, spacesuited astronauts repaired it. It was then relaunched by the arm and operated successfully for six years before falling from orbit.

Shuttle astronauts also carry out a certain amount of experimental work in orbit. Particularly much scientific work on the shuttle takes place during missions in which the scientific laboratory *Spacelab* is being carried.

▲ George Nelson carrying out an experiment into crystal growth on *Discovery* during the STS-26 shuttle mission in September 1988.

◄ On an earlier mission, 41-C in April 1984, Nelson inspects the *Solar Max* satellite, which has just been captured. He is hitching a ride on *Challenger*'s robot arm.

► Also on mission 41-C, the arm is used to place in orbit the *Long Duration Exposure Facility* (*LDEF*), carrying a host of experiments.

Humans in space

Spot facts

● The world's first space traveler was not human. She was a dog called Laika, meaning "Barker." She flew aboard the second artificial satellite, Sputnik 2, which the Soviets launched in November 1957.

● The space shuttle lavatory is flushed by air, not water, and is equipped with foot restraints and a seat belt.

● Astronauts sometimes experience flashes of light, even with their eyes closed. They are caused by cosmic rays from outer space striking the retina of the eyes.

● On December 21, 1988 cosmonauts Vladimir Titov and Musa Manarov returned to Earth after a record 365 days 22 hours in space in the Mir space station.

▶ The days when astronauts have to wear cumbersome spacesuits in orbit are long gone. For most of the time they live in "shirt-sleeve," air-conditioned comfort. Occasionally they sport some really way-out gear, as the crew did here on the STS-26 shuttle mission in 1988!

Human beings cannot by themselves survive the alien world of space. Space has no air for breathing or protection; it is full of dangerous radiation and bits of rock traveling at high speed; the temperature is either scorching hot (in sunlight) or deathly cold (in shade).

But by designing suitable transportation into orbit and living accommodations there, human beings have shown that they can live quite happily in space. They find that their bodies can tolerate the strange state of weightlessness for at least a year. And, protected in pressurized spacesuits, they can venture outside their spacecraft to "walk" and work in space: carrying out experiments and mending satellites.

Surviving the hazards

At the beginning of the Space Age no one had the remotest idea whether flesh-and-blood human beings would be able to survive the hazards of space flight. First they had to withstand the high g-forces during launch – the forces on their bodies caused by the fierce acceleration of the launch rockets. This would make their bodies up to eight times heavier than normal.

When, however, they entered orbit, the pull on their bodies would cease abruptly. They would become weightless. What effect would this have on their blood, their heart, and their other body organs? Would these organs fail?

To help them find out, space scientists subjected astronauts to high g-forces in giant centrifuges. They sent monkeys and dogs into space, first for brief suborbital trips and then into orbit and back. The results were encourag-ing. Human beings could survive high g-forces for a short time; animals could survive short periods of weightlessness.

But no one really knew what would happen to the first humans to brave the space frontier until April 12, 1961. On that day the Russian Yuri Gagarin soared into space, circled the Earth once, and returned safely to a hero's welcome. In 108 minutes this first cosmonaut traveled a distance of 40,000 km (25,000 mi.). He appeared unharmed by the g-forces and one hour of weightlessness. This gave Soviet space scientists the confidence to launch a second cosmonaut. In August Gherman Titov, aged only 25, remained in space for more than a day without coming to any harm. The break-through had been made. Space no longer appeared to be such a barrier. Humankind had begun its journey to the stars.

▲ The Soviet cosmonauts who pioneered space travel in 1961. Yuri Gagarin (right) made a one-orbit flight on April 12; Gherman Titov made 17 orbits on August 6.

▶ John Glenn enters the Mercury capsule *Friendship 7* on February 20, 1962. Within hours he will be speeding around the Earth at 28,000 km/h (over 17,000 mph). He was the first U.S. astronaut to confront and overcome the hazards of orbital space flight.

Living in orbit

In orbit objects appear to have no weight. They do not fall if you let them go. The Earth's gravity seems to have disappeared. But it is still there. The spacecraft (and everything it contains) is actually falling toward the Earth under gravity. But it is traveling so fast (28,000 km/h, or over 17,000 mph) that the Earth beneath curves away at the same rate as it is falling. In other words it stays at the same height – in orbit. This state is properly called free-fall, but is popularly termed weightlessness.

Weightlessness dominates everything you do in orbit – moving, eating, drinking, sleeping, and going to the bathroom. For example, you cannot walk in orbit, because there is nothing to hold your feet down. You cannot pour liquid from a bottle – it just stays where it is. But you can suck it through a straw, because that depends on air pressure. To sleep, you have to zip yourself into a sleeping bag and attach it to

▼ Mealtimes can be fun on the space shuttle. Mike Lounge chases a spherical globule of raspberry drink during a dinner break on shuttle mission STS-26. Astronauts Fred Hauck and Dave Hilmers look on.

something, otherwise you will just float away. Space toilets are fitted with an air-flushing system to draw wastes away from your body once they have been excreted.

The body itself is affected by the weightless state in a number of ways, some of them serious. The study of these effects and their treatment is known as space medicine. For the first few days in orbit you will probably feel sick because the balance organs in your ears cannot make sense of the new sensations. Without gravity to pump against, your heart will begin to lose muscle tissue; so will your legs. Unless you do regular exercise, your muscles will waste away, making you feel weak when you return to Earth and gravity once again. Regular exercise is essential on long space missions.

Even more serious is a progressive loss of calcium from the body, which reduces the mass and strength of the bones. However, a careful diet and a strict exercise program helps to combat these effects, allowing astronauts to remain in space for a year or more without suffering permanent body damage.

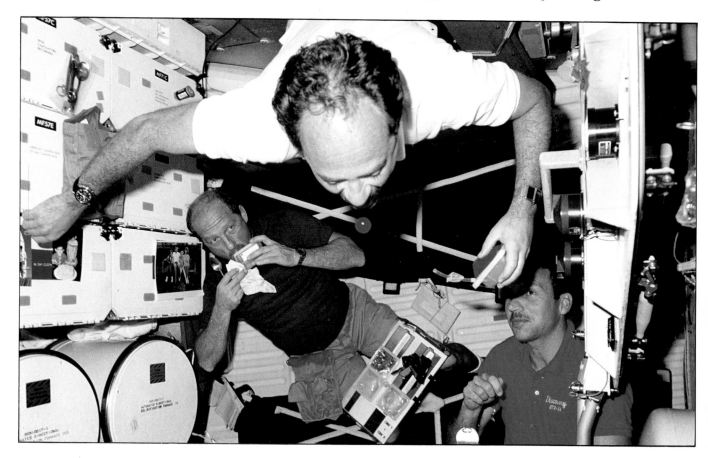

► European Space Agency astronaut Wubbo Ockels fitted out for an experiment on a "space sled" during a Spacelab mission. He will later be accelerated on the sledlike device along a track and stopped suddenly. At the same time his eyes will be subjected to different sensations and his reactions will be monitored. This experiment is designed to investigate space sickness, or space adaptation syndrome, which affects the majority of astronauts for the first few days in space.

▼ (below left) Sleeping aboard the shuttle orbiter. The sleeping quarters are on the lower deck, and comprise a number of bunks, to which the astronauts attach their sleeping bags. When they are asleep, their arms tend to float upward in the weightless conditions. If the bunks are full, astronauts attach their sleeping bags to the walls or anything suitable. Because the orbiter is quite noisy, they usually wear earplugs.

▼ (below right) Guion Bluford gets in some exercise on a treadmill during an early shuttle flight. On shuttle missions exercise is not really necessary because they seldom last longer than a week. It is on long missions in space stations that it becomes vital to do regular exercise to prevent the body muscles from wasting away.

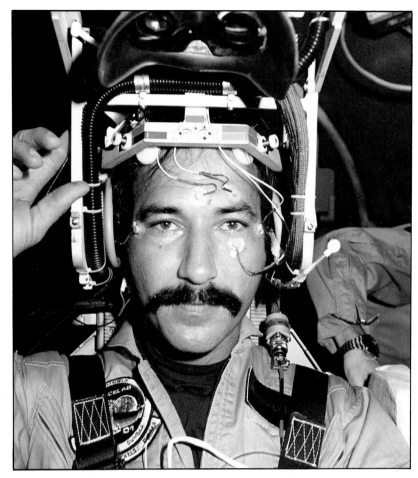

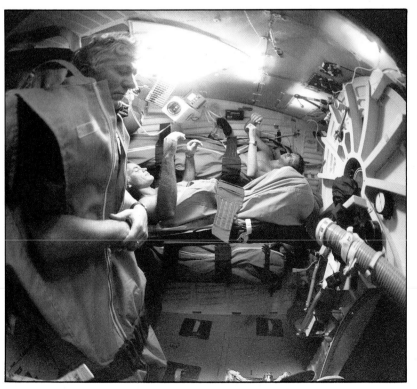

Spacesuits

On any manned spacecraft the most important system by far is the life-support system. This provides the means of keeping the astronauts alive and protecting them from space hazards.

The astronauts live in a pressurized cabin, whose metal walls act as a barrier to dangerous radiation and to micrometeoroids, tiny swift particles that stream through space. It is pressurized to atmospheric pressure. The astronauts breathe an 80/20, nitrogen/oxygen, mixture much like the air on Earth. The air is

circulated through an air-conditioning unit, which absorbs odors and the carbon dioxide the astronauts breathe out. The air is kept at a comfortable temperature and humidity.

When the astronauts leave their spacecraft to go spacewalking, they wear a spacesuit that affords them the same level of protection as their pressurized cabin. The early spacesuits, worn by the U.S. Mercury astronauts, for example, were simply modified versions of the pressure suits worn by high-flying jet pilots. When astronauts began spacewalking in the mid-1960s, specialist spacesuits were developed to offer extra protection from the direct exposure to space. They were umbilical suits, which drew oxygen from the life-support system of the spacecraft through a tube.

For the Apollo Moon-landing missions, the astronauts wore a spacesuit that was self-contained so that they were free to roam. The life-support equipment was in a backpack.

The shuttle suit, properly called an extra-vehicular mobility unit (EMU), evolved from it. It is made in two parts – trousers and top; the top part has a rigid aluminum frame and a built-in life-support backpack.

In the early days the whole spacecraft often had to be depressurized before the astronaut could open a hatch and float into space. Modern craft, however, have an airlock, a chamber inside the crew cabin which can be independently depressurized.

Astronauts enter the airlock and breathe pure oxygen for some time before they suit up. This is to clear their blood of nitrogen. Otherwise the nitrogen would bubble out when they wore their suits, which operate at reduced pressure. This would give them dangerous cramp attacks known as "the bends." When the astronauts are suited up, they depressurize the airlock, open the exit hatch, and float out into space. They become human satellites.

◀ George Nelson gets ready for the STS-26 shuttle mission in September 1988. He is wearing a newly-designed pressurized flight suit. All shuttle astronauts now wear these suits on their journey into orbit. They came into use following the *Challenger* disaster to give astronauts added protection in the event of a cabin depressurization during lift-off.

Apollo EVA suit

The spacesuit the Apollo astronauts wore on their daring EVAs ("extra-vehicular activities") on the Moon. Over the water-cooled "long johns" was a comfort layer, a pressure "bladder," and a restraint layer. On top was a 17-layer outer suit to provide protection against meteoroid particles and sunlight. A backpack carried oxygen, power, and communications equipment.

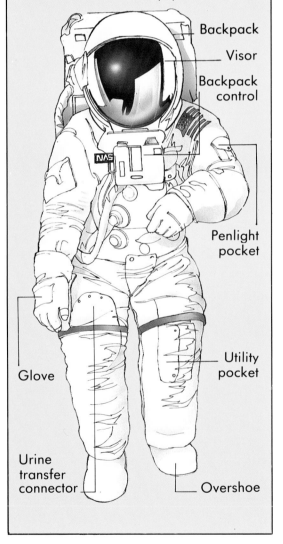

Backpack

Visor

Backpack control

NAS

Penlight pocket

Glove

Utility pocket

Urine transfer connector

Overshoe

▶ An astronaut puts on the two-part shuttle spacesuit, or EMU. Next to her skin she wears water-cooled "long johns." She steps into the trousers first, then dons the upper torso, which is fitted with a life-support backpack. Torso and trousers join together by means of an airtight seal at the waist.

Spacewalking

Astronauts began leaving the comparative safety of their spacecraft and floating in space in 1965. This extravehicular activity (EVA) has been popularly termed spacewalking. EVAs are always risky because the astronauts have only a few thin layers of fabric and plastic between them and the lethal space environment. A small rip in their spacesuit would bring an agonizing death in seconds.

Surface EVAs took place on the Moon during the Apollo missions of the late 1960s and early 1970s. The astronauts wore self-contained spacesuits and roamed far and wide across the lava plains and rugged highlands of the Moon. On the last three missions they had wheeled transport in the shape of the lunar roving vehicle, or Moon buggy.

Useful EVA in orbit did not begin until the *Skylab* space station mission of 1973. *Skylab* was damaged during launch, losing a solar panel and some vital insulation. In orbit, exposed to the Sun, it began to overheat. But the first crew ferried up to the station carried out two daring EVAs and managed to erect a sunshade over the damaged area. The mission was saved and became spectacularly successful.

Over the years since then, the long-stay residents in the Soviet Union's space stations have carried out many in-orbit EVAs to make essential repairs to their craft. Some of the EVAs have been vital. In July 1990, for example, cosmonauts Anatoli Solovyov and Aleksandr Balandin made two long EVAs on *Mir* to check and repair their Soyuz ferry craft and close a faulty reentry hatch.

Since the space shuttle was introduced, many scheduled and a few unscheduled EVAs have taken place. EVAs have been scheduled, for example, to support experiments taking place in the cargo bay. Shuttle astronauts have also made EVAs to repair satellites that have been captured from orbit. This happened with the satellite *Solar Max* in 1984 and *Leasat 3* a year later.

While working in the cargo bay, the astronauts are usually tethered to a safety line or "ride" on the orbiter's robot arm. Often they are actively involved in satellite capture, "flying" the jet-propelled backpack known as the manned maneuvering unit (MMU).

The first spacewalk

On March 18, 1965 the Russian cosmonaut Aleksei Leonov opened the airlock of his spacecraft, *Voskhod 2*, and "walked" out into space. No one had done this before. His spacewalk lasted nearly 10 minutes.

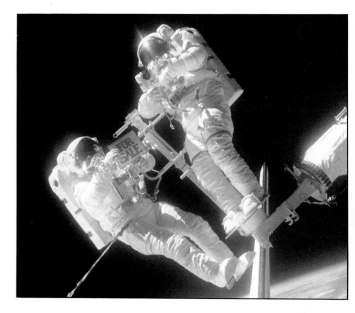

▲ (top) On shuttle mission 51-A in November 1984 astronauts Dale Gardner and Joseph Allen helped capture two communications satellites.

▶ Bruce McCandless test-flies the jet-propelled manned maneuvering unit (MMU) in February 1984 during the 41-B shuttle mission.

Space stations

Spot facts

• *The* Skylab *astronauts took along two spiders, Anita and Arabella, to see if they could spin webs in zero-gravity conditions. In fact they spun quite good webs.*

• Skylab, *launched in May 1973, fell out of orbit in July 1979, after circling the Earth 34,981 times.*

• *On the first Spacelab mission, in November 1983, Ulf Merbold from West Germany became the first foreign national to fly on a U.S. spacecraft.*

• *In December 1987 cosmonaut Yuri Romanenko returned to Earth after a record 326 days in space in the Mir space station. He was so fit that the day after landing he managed to jog for 100 m (about 100 yards).*

▶ Astronaut Jack Lousma, enjoying a shower during the second manned mission to *Skylab.* It was the first spacecraft to feature such a luxury. The problem was that, when an astronaut took a shower, fine droplets of water splashed everywhere around the cabin and had to be vacuumed up by a colleague.

In the early days of space flight astronauts did not spend a long time in space. Even the Apollo missions to the Moon took less than two weeks. The early spacecraft were too small and were not equipped for lengthy trips. There was also little room for astronauts to carry out scientific studies or experiments.

Later, bigger craft, such as the Soviet Salyuts and the U.S. *Skylab,* provided more spacious living and working accommodations for long periods. *Skylab* and the later Salyuts proved spectacularly successful. They were the first space stations. The Soviet Union's latest station, *Mir,* is being built up, module by module, into an increasingly large complex. The European-built space laboratory Spacelab has also carried out valuable work.

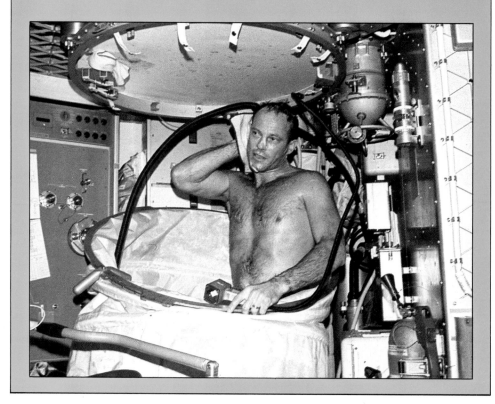

Salyut

The first space station, the Soviet Union's *Salyut 1*, was launched into orbit on April 19, 1971, and was first inhabited six weeks later by the three-man crew of *Soyuz 11*. They spent nearly 24 days in *Salyut 1*, smashing all space duration records. Tragically, they were killed when returning to Earth when their cabin accidentally depressurized at high altitude.

It was a bad start for the Salyut space-station program, which did not meet with real success until *Salyut 6* was launched in 1977. It was built of cylinders of different sizes, the biggest some 4 m (over 12 ft.) across. It measured nearly 15 m (50 ft.) long. It differed from earlier Salyuts in having two docking ports, one at each end.

In December 1977 and January 1978 two Soyuz craft flew up and docked at these ports, making the first dual linkup in space history. It showed the way ahead. A few days later, a remote-controlled cargo ship *Progress* docked automatically with *Salyut* at a port vacated by one of the Soyuz. It brought up fresh supplies of fuel, food, and mail, much welcomed.

By using automatic Progress ferries, the Soviet Union solved the problem of supporting the cosmonauts on long missions. These missions grew longer and longer – up to 140 days in 1978 and 185 days in 1980. In 1982 *Salyut 7* took over, and the space duration record continued to tumble. In 1984 came a 237-day mission – nearly eight months. And the cosmonauts still did not suffer any long-term ill effects from the prolonged weightlessness. This was good news for human space travel.

▼ A Soyuz ferry ship comes to dock with the *Salyut 1* space station. This was the first of a series of seven similarly designed Soviet space stations, launched so that cosmonauts could gain experience in living and working in space for extended periods of time.

Soyuz docks with *Salyut 1*

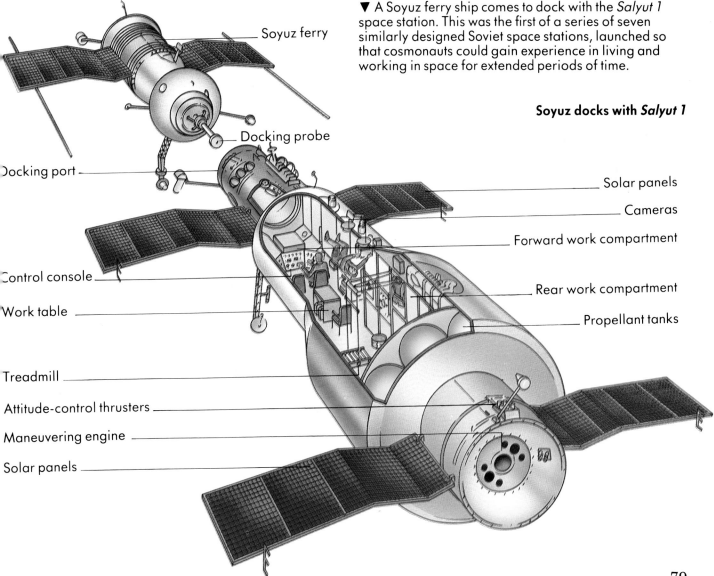

Soyuz ferry

Docking probe

Docking port

Control console

Work table

Treadmill

Attitude-control thrusters

Maneuvering engine

Solar panels

Solar panels

Cameras

Forward work compartment

Rear work compartment

Propellant tanks

Skylab

The first US space-station project, called *Skylab*, was very much a makeshift affair. It used bits of Apollo hardware, left over when the number of Moon landings was reduced. The main unit was the third stage of a Saturn V rocket, to which other units were attached.

The completed "sky laboratory" was lifted into orbit on May 14, 1973, by a Saturn V rocket. Three teams of three astronauts visited the space station over the next nine months for periods of 28, 59, and 84 days, respectively, traveling in Apollo spacecraft. They smashed all space duration records and proved that human beings could make their homes in space for long periods.

The third rocket stage formed the unit called the orbital workshop (OWS). The main living and working accommodations for the crew occupied the empty liquid-hydrogen tank of the rocket. The smaller empty liquid-oxygen tank provided storage space for waste. The upper part of the OWS led, through the airlock module, to the multiple docking adapter (MDA). This was a unit equipped with ports at which the Apollo spacecraft could dock.

▼ *Skylab* as it finally appeared in orbit, photographed by the departing third crew in February 1974 after a record-breaking 84 days in space. The picture shows the makeshift sunshields that the astronauts erected over the damaged orbital workshop.

The *Skylab* cluster

Solar instruments

Apollo telescope mount (ATM)

▶ The *Skylab* space station as it should have appeared in orbit. The solar array shown on the right was ripped away during the launch. The three-man crews were ferried up to *Skylab* in the Apollo spacecraft, shown here coming in to dock with the MDA. From end to end, the whole *Skylab* cluster measured 36 m (118 ft.) and had a mass of 85 metric tons. The OWS measured over 6.7 m (22 ft.) in diameter.

Solar array

Docking hatch

Apollo spacecraft

Docking probe

▼ The cavernous forward compartment of the orbital workshop provided plenty of room for the astronauts to carry out gymnastic feats. Here, Gerald Carr, one of the final crew members, performs for the camera.

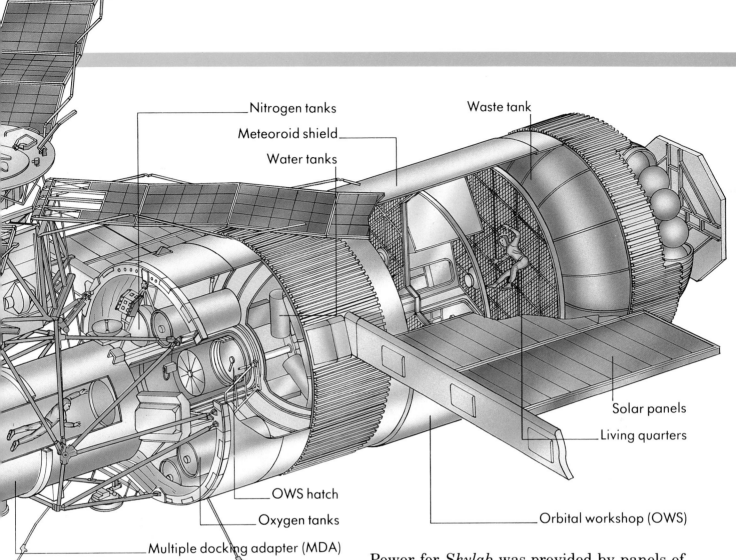

Nitrogen tanks

Meteoroid shield

Water tanks

Waste tank

Solar panels

Living quarters

OWS hatch

Oxygen tanks

Multiple docking adapter (MDA)

Orbital workshop (OWS)

▼ On the first *Skylab* visit, Dr. Joseph Kerwin inspects Charles Conrad's mouth. Medical inspections were carried out regularly on *Skylab* to monitor the effects of prolonged weightlessness.

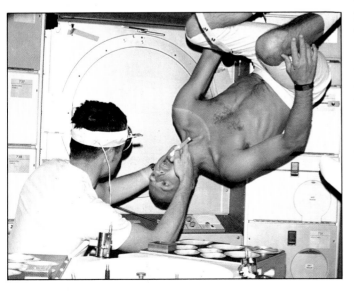

Power for *Skylab* was provided by panels of solar cells on the OWS and on a sail-like structure mounted on the MDA. This structure, which also housed a package of instruments for studying the Sun, was called the Apollo telescope mount. There should have been two solar panels on the OWS, but one was ripped off during launch. A section of insulation was also ripped off the OWS and had to be repaired by the first team of astronauts.

The astronauts had a heavy work load, carrying out all manner of observations and experiments. Their observation of the Sun produced the most spectacular results. They also carried out Earth-survey observations at different wavelengths, demonstrating the great potential of such remote sensing. In engineering, they experimented with melting and crystalizing materials to produce new compounds. All the while they used themselves as guinea pigs for space medicine experiments, to monitor how their bodies reacted to long periods of weightlessness. To help keep muscles from wasting away, they used an exercise bicycle.

Spacelab

European space science took a great leap forward in November 1983, when the space shuttle carried into orbit Spacelab, the first specialized space laboratory. Spacelab was designed and built by the European Space Agency. It fits into the cargo bay of the shuttle orbiter and remains there while in space. Like the shuttle itself, Spacelab is designed to be reusable.

There are two main units in Spacelab. One is a pressurized laboratory module, and the other is an unpressurized pallet, or platform, for carrying instruments that need to be exposed to the space environment. The standard configuration is the so-called long module and pallets, shown in the picture at far right. The long module is a two-segment cylinder about 7 m (23 ft.) long and 4 m (13 ft.) across. It contains laboratory equipment and instruments in standard-sized racks along the sides. It has a powerful computer system to analyze results on the spot. But many results are relayed to scientific centers back on Earth.

Some Spacelab investigators are professional astronauts from NASA, called mission specialists, who have a strong scientific back-

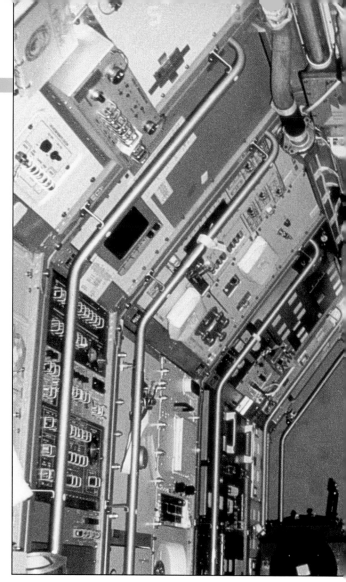

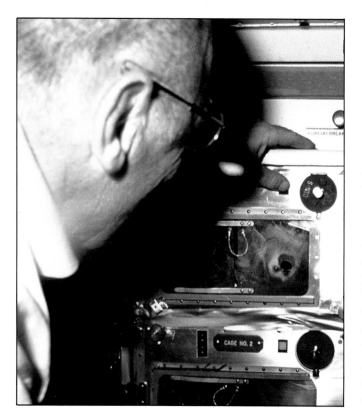

◀ Spacelab scientists carry out a variety of biological studies in orbit. On the Spacelab 3 mission, in April 1985, there were two dozen rats and a pair of squirrel monkeys as well as a human crew of seven. The scientists studied the effects on these animals of weightlessness. Here mission specialist William Thornton is observing one of the squirrel monkeys. But who is really upside-down: man or monkey?

ground. Others are nonastronaut scientists from both the United States and Europe who have particular expertise in the subjects being studied. They are known as payload specialists.

The investigators carry out experiments and observations in many branches of science and engineering. They photograph the Earth and make telescopic observations of the heavens. They study living things, from flies to monkeys, to see how they react to weightlessness. They conduct medical experiments on themselves, taking daily blood samples, for example. They also carry out tests to gain a greater insight into such problems as space adaptation syndrome, or space sickness.

▼ Spacelab in orbit some 270 km (170 mi.) above the Earth. The laboratory is shown in its common configuration of long module and pallets. Spacelab scientists only work in the laboratory; they eat and sleep in the living quarters of the orbiter, to which Spacelab is linked by a pressurized tunnel.

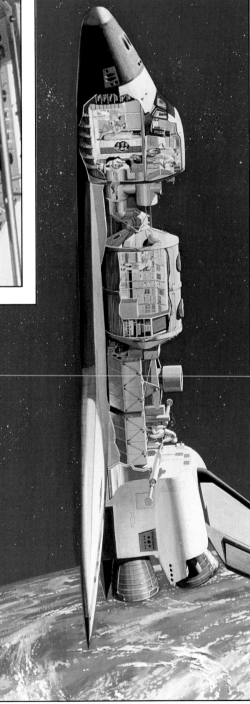

▲ European astronaut Ulf Merbold, pictured on the "ceiling" of Spacelab on its first flight in November 1983. Merbold was one of two payload specialists.

▼ A busy scene on board Spacelab during the mission of October 1985, dedicated to West Germany. The crew of eight included Guion Bluford (U.S., left) and Reinhard Furrer (West Germany).

Mir

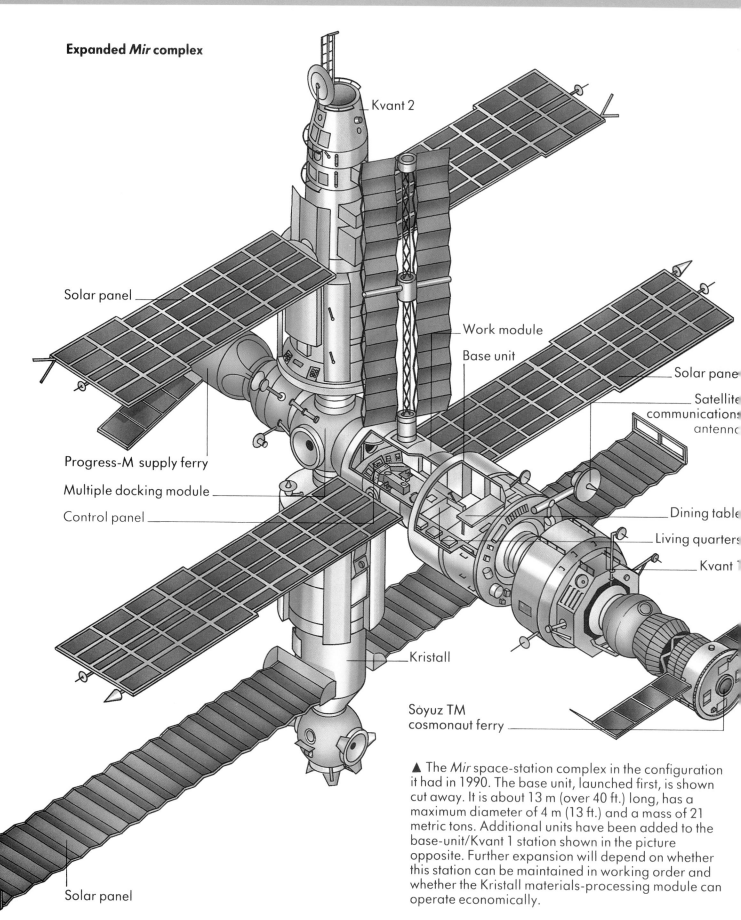

Expanded *Mir* complex

Kvant 2

Solar panel

Work module

Base unit

Solar pane

Satellit
communications
antenn

Progress-M supply ferry

Multiple docking module

Control panel

Dining table

Living quarters

Kvant 1

Kristall

Sóyuz TM
cosmonaut ferry

Solar panel

▲ The *Mir* space-station complex in the configuration
it had in 1990. The base unit, launched first, is shown
cut away. It is about 13 m (over 40 ft.) long, has a
maximum diameter of 4 m (13 ft.) and a mass of 21
metric tons. Additional units have been added to the
base-unit/Kvant 1 station shown in the picture
opposite. Further expansion will depend on whether
this station can be maintained in working order and
whether the Kristall materials-processing module can
operate economically.

The Soviet Union launched seven Salyut space stations between 1971 and 1982. In February 1986 it launched a new design called *Mir* (meaning "Peace"), which is still in orbit. The craft looks similar to the later Salyuts but is in fact quite different. For one thing the interior is much more spacious. It provides mainly living space for the crew, with separate cabins for each person. It is not cluttered, like the Salyuts, with experimental equipment.

Outside, the main new feature of *Mir* is a spherical docking module at the front end, with five docking ports. There is also a single docking port at the other end, making six in all. This design has allowed *Mir* to be expanded.

The first add-on unit docked automatically with the rear port in April 1987. It was called Kvant, after the physics term "quantum". In fact it is now called Kvant 1, because in December 1989 a large unit called the Re-equipment Module, or Kvant 2, docked at the other end. It was later repositioned to a side port of the docking module.

Kvant 2 is, at 13.7 m (45 ft.), a meter longer

▲ The *Mir* space station in July 1987, as photographed by the crew of the departing *Soyuz TM-2*. By then the base unit had been expanded by the addition of the Kvant 1 module, in place since April. Docked with Kvant 1 in the picture is the newly arrived *Soyuz TM-3*.

than the base unit itself. It houses an experimental compartment, an airlock and a shower, the first on board *Mir*. It also carried up to *Mir* the first model of the Soviet version of the American MMU, or manned maneuvering unit. This jet-propelled backpack, named Icarus, runs on compressed air. It is used for inspecting and repairing the *Mir* complex.

A third module, the Kristall materials-processing module, docked with the complex at the port opposite Kvant 2 in 1990. It is described as a mini-factory that is intended to produce flawless semiconductor crystals for use in electronics and ultrapure drugs for use in medicine. The manufactured materials would be returned to Earth periodically by unmanned Soyuz-type craft.

Units of measurement

Units of measurement

This encyclopedia gives measurements in metric units, which are commonly used in science. Approximate equivalents in traditional American units, sometimes called U.S. customary units, are also given in the text, in parentheses.

Some common metric and U.S. units

Here are some equivalents, accurate to parts per million. For many practical purposes rougher equivalents may be adequate, especially when the quantity being converted from one system to the other is known with an accuracy of just one or two digits. Equivalents marked with an asterisk (*) are exact.

Volume
1 cubic centimeter = 0.0610237 cubic inch
1 cubic meter = 35.3147 cubic feet
1 cubic meter = 1.30795 cubic yards
1 cubic kilometer = 0.239913 cubic mile

1 cubic inch = 16.3871 cubic centimeters
1 cubic foot = 0.0283168 cubic meter
1 cubic yard = 0.764555 cubic meter

Liquid measure
1 milliliter = 0.0338140 fluidounce
1 liter = 1.05669 quarts

1 fluidounce = 29.5735 milliliters
1 quart = 0.946353 liter

Mass and weight
1 gram = 0.0352740 ounce
1 kilogram = 2.20462 pounds
1 metric ton = 1.10231 short tons

1 ounce = 28.3495 grams
1 pound = 0.453592 kilogram
1 short ton = 0.907185 metric ton

Length
1 millimeter = 0.0393701 inch
1 centimeter = 0.393701 inch
1 meter = 3.28084 feet
1 meter = 1.09361 yards
1 kilometer = 0.621371 mile

1 inch = 2.54* centimeters
1 foot = 0.3048* meter
1 yard = 0.9144* meter
1 mile = 1.60934 kilometers

Area
1 square centimeter = 0.155000 square inch
1 square meter = 10.7639 square feet
1 square meter = 1.19599 square yards
1 square kilometer = 0.386102 square mile

1 square inch = 6.4516* square centimeters
1 square foot = 0.0929030 square meter
1 square yard = 0.836127 square meter
1 square mile = 2.58999 square kilometers

1 hectare = 2.47105 acres
1 acre = 0.404686 hectare

Temperature conversions

To convert temperatures in degrees Celsius to temperatures in degrees Fahrenheit, or vice versa, use these formulas:

Celsius Temperature = (Fahrenheit Temperature − 32) × 5/9
Fahrenheit Temperature = (Celsius Temperature × 9/5) + 32

Numbers and abbreviations

Numbers

Scientific measurements sometimes involve extremely large numbers. Scientists often express large numbers in a concise "exponential" form using powers of 10. The number one billion, or 1,000,000,000, if written in this form, would be 10^9; three billion, or 3,000,000,000, would be 3×10^9. The "exponent" 9 tells you that there are nine zeros following the 3. More complicated numbers can be written in this way by using decimals; for example, 3.756×10^9 is the same as 3,756,000,000.

Very small numbers – numbers close to zero – can be written in exponential form with a minus sign on the exponent. For example, one-billionth, which is 1/1,000,000,000 or 0.000000001, would be 10^{-9}. Here, the 9 in the exponent -9 tells you that, in the decimal form of the number, the 1 is in the ninth place to the right of the decimal point. Three-billionths, or 3/1,000,000,000, would be 3×10^{-9}; accordingly, 3.756×10^{-9} would mean 0.000000003756 (or 3.756/1,000,000,000).

Here are the American names of some powers of ten, and how they are written in numerals:

1 million (10^6)	1,000,000
1 billion (10^9)	1,000,000,000
1 trillion (10^{12})	1,000,000,000,000
1 quadrillion (10^{15})	1,000,000,000,000,000
1 quintillion (10^{18})	1,000,000,000,000,000,000
1 sextillion (10^{21})	1,000,000,000,000,000,000,000
1 septillion (10^{24})	1,000,000,000,000,000,000,000,000

Principal abbreviations used in the encyclopedia

°C	degrees Celsius	kg	kilogram
cc	cubic centimeter	l	liter
cm	centimeter	lb.	pound
cu.	cubic	m	meter
d	days	mi.	mile
°F	degrees Fahrenheit	ml	milliliter
fl. oz.	fluidounce	mm	millimeter
fps	feet per second	mph	miles per hour
ft.	foot	mps	miles per second
g	gram	mya	millions of years ago
h	hour	N	north
Hz	hertz	oz.	ounce
in.	inch	qt.	quart
K	kelvin (degree temperature)	s	second
		S	south
		sq.	square
		V	volt
		y	year
		yd.	yard

Glossary

aerodynamics The study of the behavior of air flowing past objects and of objects moving through the air.

air brakes The kind of brakes trucks and trains commonly have; compressed air is used to apply the brakes.

air-cushion vehicle A vehicle that glides over the surface of land or water on a layer, or "cushion," of compressed air. A hovercraft is an air-cushion vehicle.

airfoil The shape of an aircraft wing: broad in front, sharp behind, curved on top, and flat underneath. This shape develops lift when it moves through the air.

airframe The body structure of an aircraft.

airlock A chamber in a spacecraft from which the air can be removed. Astronauts pass through an airlock before and after spacewalking.

airship A lighter-than-air craft that gets its lift from a light gas, usually helium these days.

articulated truck A tractor-trailer – a combination of truck engine and trailer, joined by a flexible coupling.

artificial satellite Usually just called satellite; a human-made object that circles the Earth in orbit.

astronaut A person who travels in space. The Russian term for an astronaut is "cosmonaut".

astronautics The science of space travel.

atmosphere The layer of gases around the Earth or heavenly body.

attitude The position of a spacecraft in relation to something else, for example the horizon.

blimp An airship that does not have a rigid frame.

booster The first stage of a multistage rocket, or an additional rocket unit added to a rocket to give it extra lift on takeoff.

bullet train A very fast, highly streamlined train, particularly one on Japan's Shinkansen network.

capsule The cramped crew compartment of early spacecraft like Vostok and Mercury.

chassis A rigid frame on which a body is built; used in building trucks and a few cars.

clutch Part of the power train of a car, truck, or motorcycle. It disconnects the engine from the transmission when the driver or rider wishes to change gear.

commercial vehicle One used in commerce, for example trucks for carrying goods, and buses for carrying passengers.

communications satellite A satellite used to relay radio signals from one place on Earth to another.

compression ignition The principle on which the diesel engine works. The fuel is ignited in the engine cylinders by the heat developed by high compression of the air taken in.

container A standard-sized box in which goods are carried. Containers are carried by truck, train, and ship and can be transferred readily from one to the other.

cosmic rays Penetrating electrically charged atomic particles that stream through space.

cosmonaut The Russian term for an astronaut.

countdown The counting down of time before a rocket is launched.

delta wing An aircraft wing shaped like the Greek capital letter delta.

derailleur gears Bicycle gears that work by shifting the chain between sprocket wheels of different sizes.

diesel engine An engine that runs on a diesel fuel. It is called a compression-ignition engine because fuel is ignited in the cylinders by hot, highly compressed air.

diesel-electric The most common form of diesel locomotive, in which the engine drives an electricity generator. The electricity produced is then fed to electric motors to turn the wheels.

differential A system of gears in the power train of a car or truck, which allows the drive wheels to turn at different speeds when the vehicle turns a corner.

dirigible An early name for an airship. The word means "steerable": a balloon that can be steered rather than just drifting.

docking The linking up of two spacecraft in orbit.

drag The resistance a body experiences when traveling through the air or water.

drive shaft A long shaft in cars with rear-wheel drive which carries motion from the transmission to the final drive.

ELV Expendable launch vehicle; one that can be used only once.

encounter The meeting in space between a space probe and its target.

epicyclic gear Also called sun-and-planet gear; the kind of gear system used in the hub gear of a bicycle. It has small gear wheels (planets) revolving around a larger central gear wheel (sun) inside a toothed ring (annulus).

ESA The European Space Agency, the coordinating body for space activities in Western Europe.

escape velocity The speed at which a body must travel to escape from the gravitational attraction of the Earth or another body.

EVA Extravehicular activity; activity outside a spacecraft, commonly termed spacewalking.

extraterrestrial Existing outside the Earth.

final drive The final part in an automotive power train. It includes the differential, which drives the half-axles that turn the drive wheels.

flyby An encounter in which a space probe flies past a planet or moon without landing.

flywheel A heavy wheel on an engine crankshaft which helps smooth out the motion imparted by the pistons.

four-stroke cycle The operating cycle of most gasoline and diesel engines, marked by the strokes (movements up and down) of the pistons in the cylinders. The strokes are intake, compression, power, and exhaust.

freighter A ship or aircraft that carries freight, or goods.

free-fall The state that exists in orbit, in which objects are falling toward the Earth but remain at the same height, because the Earth is curving away from them at the same rate. The popular name for this state is weightlessness.

fuel cell A power source used on the space shuttle, in which electricity is produced when hydrogen combines with oxygen to form water.

funicular A mountain railway system in which two cars work together, one traveling up while the other travels down.

fuselage The main body of an aircraft.

gantry The tower that gives access to a rocket on the launchpad.

gas turbine An engine that burns fuel to make hot gases which spin a turbine to produce power.

gauge The distance between the rails of a railroad track. The standard gauge is 143.5 cm (4 ft., 8½ in.).

geostationary orbit An orbit 35,900 km (22,300 mi.) high, in which a satellite takes just 24 hours to circle the Earth. In such an orbit above the Equator a satellite appears to be fixed in the sky.

g-forces The extra forces set up by a rocket or a spacecraft when it accelerates or decelerates.

gravity The force of attraction between any two bodies. It increases when the mass of the bodies increases or the distance between them decreases.

gravity assist A technique used by space probes, in which they use the gravitational attraction of a planet to increase their speed.

heat shield An outer layer on a spacecraft which protects it from the heat set up by air friction when the craft reenters the Earth's atmosphere at high speed.

hovercraft A craft that glides over a surface on a "cushion" of compressed air. A kind of air-cushion vehicle.

hydraulic brakes Ones that work by the application of liquid pressure.

hydrofoil An underwater "wing," shaped like an airfoil, which develops lift when it travels through the water.

hypersonic Traveling at five or more times the speed of sound (Mach 5).

interplanetary Between planets.

interstellar Between stars.

jet engine An engine which uses a

stream of hot gases for propulsion, with the oxygen needed for combustion being taken from the atmosphere.

jettison Throw away, or discard.

jumbo jet A wide-bodied jet airliner capable of carrying hundreds of passengers, such as the Boeing 747.

jump jet A jet plane that can take off and land vertically.

launch vehicle A rocket or system of rockets designed to launch a spacecraft into space.

launch window The period during which a spacecraft can be launched so as to reach its intended target.

life-support system The system in a manned spacecraft which enables the crew to live comfortably in space.

lift An upward force developed when an airfoil moves through the air, or a hydrofoil moves through water.

light-year The distance light travels in a year, some 10 trillion km (nearly 6 trillion mi.).

liner A ship designed to carry passengers in comfort.

lunar Relating to the Moon.

Mach number A measure of the speed of an aircraft. The number signifies the speed compared with the local speed of sound (which varies with altitude); for example Mach 2 means twice the speed of sound.

manned maneuvering unit (MMU) A jet-propelled backpack used by space shuttle astronauts when spacewalking.

meteoroid A rock particle that travels through space. If it burns up in the Earth's atmosphere, we see it in the night sky as a meteor. If it is big enough, it may survive to reach the ground, where it is called a meteorite.

mission A space flight.

mission control The control center for a space flight, such as the U.S. Mission Control at the Johnson Space Center, Houston, Texas.

mission specialist One of the three types of astronauts who fly aboard the space shuttle. He or she carries out mission objectives, such as launching satellites, but does not fly the craft.

mock-up A full-size model of something, for example a dummy spacecraft in which astronauts train for a space flight.

module A major unit of a spacecraft.

moped A low-powered motorbike with pedals.

multistage rocket A rocket having two or more propulsion units, or stages, each one burning after the one in back of it has used up its propellant.

NASA The National Aeronautics and Space Administration, the body in the United States which coordinates space activities.

newton A unit of force: 1 newton is the force that will give a mass of 1 kg (2.2 lb.) an acceleration of 1 m (3.28 ft.) per second per second.

nuclear power Power produced by harnessing the heat given out when certain atoms (usually uranium) split, or undergo fission.

orbit The path in space taken by a satellite circling around the Earth, or of any small body circling around a larger one.

orbital velocity The speed a body needs to remain in orbit. The orbital velocity around the Earth at a height of about 300 km (nearly 200 mi.) is about 28,000 km/h (17,400 mph).

orbiter A spacecraft designed to circle around a planet or moon;

specifically, the space shuttle orbiter.

oxidizer The propellant in a rocket that provides oxygen.

PAM Payload-assist module, an additional rocket stage attached to some satellites which is fired to boost them to high orbit.

pantograph A spring-held arm on, for example, an electric locomotive that makes contact with a conductor wire and picks up current.

payload The "cargo" a launch vehicle or rocket carries.

payload specialist One of the three types of astronauts who fly on the space shuttle. They are scientists or engineers included in the crew to carry out experiments.

pilot astronaut One of the three classes of astronauts aboard the space shuttle, whose prime job is to fly the craft.

pinion A small gear wheel.

pneumatic tire One filled with air.

probe A spacecraft that escapes from the Earth to explore the Moon, the planets, or other bodies.

propellant A substance burned in a rocket to produce the gases that provide propulsion.

propeller A screwlike device used to propel ships and some aircraft. It has specially curved blades that develop thrust when they rotate.

power train The system in a motor vehicle that carries power from the engine to the drive wheels.

rack A toothed rod or rail used, for example, in the rack-and-pinion steering system of many cars. Rotating a meshed pinion makes the rack move from side to side.

radar A method of detecting aircraft in the air by bouncing radio waves

off them. The word stands for "radio detection and ranging."

redundancy The duplication of essential parts in a spacecraft so if one fails, another can take over.

reentry The period when a spacecraft reenters the Earth's atmosphere after a space flight.

remote sensing The gathering of data from a distance, particularly imaging data from Earth-survey satellites such as Landsat and SPOT.

retrobraking Firing a rocket in the direction of travel so as to slow down a spacecraft. This is carried out to bring a spacecraft down from orbit or to slow it for a soft landing.

rocket One type of engine that is propelled by a stream of gases escaping from the rear. Reaction to these gases escaping backward produces thrust to propel the rocket forward. Unlike a jet, a rocket is a self-contained engine, which carries not only fuel but also oxygen to burn the fuel.

rotary wing The rotor of a helicopter, which provides lift and propulsive thrust when it rotates.

RTG Radioisotope thermoelectric generator; a device that converts the heat of decay of a radioactive substance (usually plutonium) into electricity. Sometimes called a nuclear battery.

satellite A small body that circles in space around a larger one. Many of the planets have natural satellites, or moons; the Earth now has many artificial satellites.

shaft drive A method of power transmission in some motorcycles that uses a shaft rather than the usual chain to link the engine and the rear wheel.

shock absorber A kind of piston device in the suspension system of a car or motorcycle to stop the body from bouncing too much after going over a bump.

simulator A realistic model, such as a mock-up of a spacecraft, that behaves like the real thing; used by astronauts during training.

snorkel A tube device used in submarines to let air into the vessel while it is still submerged.

solar Relating to the Sun.

solar cell An electric cell that converts the energy in sunlight into electricity; used to power most satellites.

Solar System The Sun's family in space, including the planets, moons, asteroids, meteoroids, and comets.

solar wind The stream of charged particles given off by the Sun.

sonic boom A noise like a thunderclap produced when an aircraft travels at more than the speed of sound.

sound barrier It was once thought that no aircraft could travel faster than the speed of sound without breaking up, and this led to the expression "the sound barrier."

sound, speed of At sea level it is about 1,220 km/h (760 mph). It varies with altitude, becoming less as the air becomes less dense.

space medicine The study of the human body in space, particularly with regard to weightlessness.

spacewalking The popular term for extravehicular activity, or EVA.

spark ignition The principle on which the gasoline engine works. The fuel-and-air mixture drawn into the engine cylinders is ignited by a high-voltage electric spark from the spark plugs.

sprocket A toothed wheel in the chain drive of a bicycle or motorcycle.

stage One of the rocket units in a multistage rocket.

stellar Relating to the stars.

STOL Abbreviation for "short takeoff and landing." It describes aircraft with this capability.

streamlining Designing aircraft, land vehicles, and vessels with flowing lines so that they can slip more readily through the air or water.

submarine A vessel designed to travel underwater. Large submarines are used only by the world's navies.

submersible A small submarine used to support diving operations and oceanic research work.

suborbital A flight that takes a spacecraft up into space without going into orbit.

subsonic Traveling at less than the speed of sound.

supersonic Traveling at more than the speed of sound.

surface skimmers A term often applied to surface-skimming vessels, such as the hovercraft and hydrofoil.

swing-wing Or variable-geometry wing; an aircraft design in which the wings can be moved into different positions to suit the speed of flight.

telemetry The transmission of measurement data over a distance, as between a spacecraft and ground control.

terrestrial Relating to the Earth.

TGV Abbreviation for "Train à Grande Vitesse," France's high-speed train.

thrust The pushing effect of a rocket, measured in newtons, kilograms, or pounds.

thruster A small rocket engine used for maneuvering in space.

tracking Following the path of a satellite or a probe through space.

trajectory The path of a moving object, for example the flight path of a spacecraft.

transmission The unit in a power train that provides different gearing so that a vehicle can be driven at different speeds for a given engine speed.

turbocharger A turbine-driven pump that forces more air into an engine so as to increase its power.

turbofan A kind of jet engine used in aircraft which has a huge fan in the air intake. This drives air around as well as through the engine, which produces a more efficient propulsive jet.

turbojet The simplest kind of turbine-equipped engine used in aircraft. Its thrust comes wholly from an exiting jet of burned gases.

turboprop A kind of jet engine in which the jet exhaust spins a turbine that turns a propeller. Engine thrust comes both from the propeller and the jet exhaust.

UFO Unidentified flying object; an object whose presence in the sky cannot at first readily be explained. Some people believe that some UFOs are reconnaissance craft from an extraterrestrial civilization.

umbilical The tube/tether of an early spacesuit that connected it with an on-board life-support system.

VTOL Abbreviation for "vertical takeoff and landing." It describes aircraft with this capability.

weightlessness The popular term for the state that exists in orbit, where nothing appears to have any weight. The proper term is free-fall.

zero-g No gravity; another term for weightlessness.

Index

Further reading

Apfel, Necia H. *Space Station*. New York: Franklin Watts, 1987.

Berger, Melvin. *Space Shots, Shuttles, and Satellites*. New York: Putnam, 1984.

Berliner, Don. *Helicopters*. Minneapolis, Minn.: Lerner, 1983.

Boyne, Walter. *The Smithsonian Book of Flight for Young People*. New York: Atheneum/Macmillan, 1988.

Branley, Franklyn M. *Mysteries of Life on Earth and Beyond*. New York: Lodestar/Dutton, 1987.

Ford, Barbara. *The Automobile (Inventions That Changed Our Lives)*. New York: Walker & Company, 1987.

Fox, Mary Virginia. *Women Astronauts: Aboard the Shuttle*. New York: Messner, 1987.

Graham, Ian. *Submarines*. New York: Gloucester Press/Watts, 1989.

Graham, Ian. *Transportation*. New York: Hampstead Press/Watts, 1989.

Gray, Michael. *Ships and Submarines*. New York: Franklin Watts, 1986.

Herda, D. J. *Research Satellites*. New York: Franklin Watts, 1987.

Kaufman, John. *Voyager: A Flight Around the World*. Hillside, N.J.: Enslow, 1989.

Kerrod, Robin. *Motorcycles*. New York: Gloucester Press/Watts, 1989.

Kerrod, Robin. *A Space Station*. New York: Warwick Press/Watts, 1988.

Lambert, Mark. *Aircraft Technology*. New York: Bookwright Press/Watts, 1990.

McKissack, Patricia, and Frederick McKissack. *A Long Hard Journey*. New York: Walker & Company, 1989.

Pizer, Vernon. *The Irrepressible Automobile: A Freewheeling Jaunt Through the Fascinating World of the Motorcar*. New York: Dodd, Mead, 1986.

Pollard, Michael. *From Cycle to Spaceship: The Story of Transport*. New York: Facts on File, 1987.

Smith, Howard E. *Daring the Unknown: A History of NASA*. New York: Gulliver/Harcourt Brace Jovanovich, 1987.

Sullivan, George. *Famous Blimps and Airships*. New York: Dodd, Mead/Puttnam, 1988.

White, Jack R. *Satellites of Today and Tomorrow*. New York: Dodd, Mead, 1985.

Picture Credits

N